THE U.S. NAVAL INSTITUTE ON
NAVAL LEADERSHIP

In the U.S. Navy, "Wheel Books" were once found in the uniform pockets of every junior and many senior petty officers. Each small notebook was unique to the Sailor carrying it, but all had in common a collection of data and wisdom that the individual deemed useful in the effective execution of his or her duties. Often used as a substitute for experience among neophytes and as a portable library of reference information for more experienced personnel, those weathered pages contained everything from the time of the next tide, to leadership hints from a respected chief petty officer, to the color coding of the phone-and-distance line used in underway replenishments.

In that same tradition, U.S. Naval Institute Wheel Books provide supplemental information, pragmatic advice, and cogent analysis on topics important to all naval professionals. Drawn from the U.S. Naval Institute's vast archives, the series combines articles from the Institute's flagship publication *Proceedings*, as well as selections from the oral history collection and from Naval Institute Press books, to create unique guides on a wide array of fundamental professional subjects.

THE U.S. NAVAL INSTITUTE ON
NAVAL LEADERSHIP

EDITED BY THOMAS J. CUTLER

NAVAL INSTITUTE PRESS
Annapolis, Maryland

Naval Institute Press
291 Wood Road
Annapolis, MD 21402

© 2015 by the U.S. Naval Institute
All rights reserved. No part of this book may be reproduced or utilized in any form or by any means, electronic or mechanical, including photocopying and recording, or by any information storage and retrieval system, without permission in writing from the publisher.

Library of Congress Cataloging-in-Publication data is available.

♾ Print editions meet the requirements of ANSI/NISO z39.48–1992 (Permanence of Paper). Printed in the United States of America.

23 22 21 20 19 18 17 16 15   9 8 7 6 5 4 3 2 1
First printing

CONTENTS

Editor's Note xi

Introduction 1

1 "Leadership for Young Officers at Sea" 7
 (Selection from chapter 1 of *Saltwater Leadership*)
 Rear Admiral Robert O. Wray Jr., USN

2 "Leadership: The Theory Behind the Principles" 15
 Major Thomas U. Wall, USMC

3 "The Profession of Leading" 29
 (From the U. S. Naval Institute blog)
 Captain David Tyler, USN

4 "The Naval Officer: Manager or Leader?" 31
 Lieutenant R. T. E. Bowler III, USN, and
 Lieutenant D. R. Bowler, USN

5 "Young Officers and Leadership" 41
 Admiral Arleigh Burke, USN (Ret.)

6 "The Challenge of Moral Leadership" 43
 Captain Michael J. O'Hara, USMC

7 "Closing the Gaps in Naval Leadership" 53
   Lieutenant James Stavridis, USN

8 "Leadership: Some Soundings" 61
   Lieutenant Thomas F. Marfiak, USN

9 "Bring Back Humility" 68
   Senior Chief Jim Murphy, USN (Ret.)

10 "Military Leadership" 71
   Captain E. F. Carlson, USMC

11 "Leadership: Above and Beyond Management" 73
   Lieutenant Commander Robert A. Fliegel, USN

12 "Petty Officers" and "Leadership, Discipline, and
   Personal Relations" 81
   (Selections from chapters 1 and 5 of *The Bluejacket's Manual*, 1st and 24th editions)
   Lieutenant Ridley McLean, USN, and Thomas J. Cutler

13 "Successful Leadership" 87
   (Selection from chapter 18 of *The Naval Officer's Guide*, 12th edition)
   Commander Lesa A. McComas, USN (Ret.)

14 "Leadership" 94
   (Selection from chapter 16 of *The Marine Officer's Guide*, 7th edition)
   Lieutenant Colonel Kenneth Estes, USMC (Ret.)

15 "Advice for Midshipmen" 113
   (Selection from chapter 20 of *Career Compass*)
   Rear Admiral James A. Winnefeld Sr., USN (Ret.)

16 "Leadership: The Core of What We Do" 121
   (Selection from chapter 1 of *Newly Commissioned
   Naval Officer's Guide*)
   Commander Fred W. Kacher, USN

17 "Leading Sailors" 132
   (Selection from chapter 2 of *The Professional Naval Officer*)
   Rear Admiral James A. Winnefeld Sr., USN (Ret.)

18 "The Tuned-In Leader" 145
   Ensign Robert Van Winter, USN

19 "So You Want to Be a Department Head" 151
   Lieutenant Commander Fred W. Kacher, USN

20 "On Leading Snipes" 157
   Lieutenant Jim Stavridis, USN

21 "Know Your Men . . . Know Your Business . . .
   Know Yourself" 163
   Major C. A. Bach, USA

22 "Outcomes, Essences, and Individuals" 174
   Lieutenant Thomas B. Grassey, USNR

23 "Dissidence Is Not a Virtue" 184
   Admiral Arleigh Burke, USN (Ret.)

   Conclusion 195

   Index 197

EDITOR'S NOTE

Because this book is an anthology, containing documents from different time periods, the selections included here are subject to varying styles and conventions. Other variables are introduced by the evolving nature of the Naval Institute's publication practices. For those reasons, certain editorial decisions were required in order to avoid introducing confusion or inconsistencies and to expedite the process of assembling these sometimes disparate pieces.

Gender

Most jarring of the differences that readers will encounter are likely those associated with gender. Many of the included selections were written when the armed forces were primarily a male domain and so adhere to purely masculine references. I have chosen to leave the original language intact in these documents for the sake of authenticity and to avoid the complications that can arise when trying to make anachronistic adjustments. So readers are asked to "translate" (converting the ubiquitous "he" to "he or she" and "his" to "her or his" as required) and, while doing so, to celebrate the progress that we have made in these matters in more recent times.

Author "Biographies"

Another problem arises when considering biographical information of the various authors whose works make up this special collection. Some of the selections included in this anthology were originally accompanied by biographical information about their authors. Others were not. Those "biographies" that do exist vary a great deal in terms of length and depth, some amounting to a single sentence pertaining to the author's current duty station, others consisting of several paragraphs that cover the author's career. Varying degrees of research—some quite time consuming and some yielding no results—are required to find biographical information from other sources. Because of these uneven variables, and because as a general rule we are more interested in what these authors have to say more than who they are or were, I have chosen to even the playing field by foregoing accompanying "biographies."

Readers will recognize some authors by their famous names (Arleigh Burke as an obvious example) and others will make their own connections. Some will likely recognize Lieutenant Tom Grassey as the future editor of the *Naval War College Review*. The Bowler brothers are the sons of Commander R. T. E. Bowler Jr., secretary-treasurer (CEO equivalent) of the Naval Institute for many years. Lieutenant Tom Marfiak later became a Naval Institute CEO after retiring from the Navy as a rear admiral, and many will recognize Senior Chief Jim Murphy as a current frequent contributor to *Proceedings*.

Ranks

I have retained the ranks of the authors *at the time of their publication*. As noted above, some of the authors wrote early in their careers. Although a sidelight to the intent of this volume, it is nonetheless interesting to see a piece written by Admiral Jim Stavridis when he was a lieutenant. It says much about the individuals, about the significance of the Naval Institute's forum, and about the importance of writing to the naval services—something that is sometimes underappreciated.

Other Anomalies

Readers may detect some inconsistencies in editorial style, reflecting staff changes at the Naval Institute, evolving practices in publishing itself, and various other factors not always identifiable. Some of the selections will include citational support, others will not. Authors sometimes coined their own words and occasionally violated traditional style conventions. *Bottom line:* with the exception of the removal of some extraneous materials (such as section numbers from book excerpts) and the conversion to a consistent font and overall design, these articles and excerpts appear as they originally did when first published.

INTRODUCTION

In the plotting room far below, Ensign Merdinger got a call to send up some men to fill in for the killed and wounded. Many of the men obviously wanted to go—it looked like a safer bet than suffocating in the plotting room. Others wanted to stay—they preferred to keep a few decks between themselves and the bombs. Merdinger picked them at random, and he could see in some faces an almost pleading look to be included in the other group, whichever it happened to be. But no one murmured a word, and his orders were instantly obeyed. Now he understood more clearly the reasons for the system of discipline, the drills, the little rituals . . . all the things that made the Navy essentially autocratic but at the same time made it work.—Walter Lord, *Day of Infamy*

The scene described here actually took place on board the battleship *Nevada* during the Japanese attack on Pearl Harbor at the beginning of World War II. Besides its dramatic appeal, this glimpse of history illustrates one of the unique characteristics of military organizations. The Sailors in *Nevada*'s plotting room did not carry out their orders because they wanted to, or because they were seeking a bonus in their paycheck. They did what Ensign Merdinger directed because their fears and sense of self-preservation were overruled by the system of discipline that is an essential component of any military organization.

That is as it should be, and no one who has faced the extreme challenges that sometimes come with naval service—whether "from the dangers of the sea or the violence of the enemy"—will deny that an extreme form of discipline is a necessary component of military service. There are times when a leader must rely on his or her authority to get subordinates to do what needs to be done, even at great peril.

The rigors of basic training or plebe summer and the fear of punishments described in the UCMJ are some of the components of that system of discipline that must sometimes be relied upon in times of emergency. But life-and-death situations are not everyday occurrences, even in a life at sea. Consequently, leaders must reserve (and conserve) that unique authority for those extraordinary times when it is needed.

For those other times, when routine is dominant, that system of authority must be supplemented and reinforced by relevant and constructive practices that are more subtle and complex. The "leader" who relies on authority alone is no leader. True leaders—or those who aspire to be—understand that the authority that comes with their gold braid or chevrons is merely a foundation on which to build, but it cannot stand alone. What we generically call "leadership" is the resultant structure that we build on that foundation of decreed authority, a structure that consists of elements of pragmatism and of philosophy, one that ranges from simple to complex and is a topic that never loses its relevance or its allure.

A Worthwhile Quest

What makes this subject endure is, first of all, its importance: leadership is one of the core components of military capability, enhanced and sustained by the realization that there are few more rewarding—or more challenging—undertakings than to be given the privilege—and the responsibility—of leading others.

But what also keeps leadership alive as a fresh topic is its elusiveness. Simply defining leadership can be problematic. Definitions range from the simple "The art of accomplishing the Navy's mission through people" (from *Naval*

Terms Dictionary: 4th Ed., by John V. Noel and Edward L. Beach) to the more complicated "Leadership is leaders acting—as well as caring, inspiring, and persuading others to act—for certain shared goals that represent the values—the wants and needs, the aspirations and expectations—of themselves and the people they represent" (from *Leadership* by James MacGregor Burns as quoted in the more recent *The Architecture of Leadership* by Donald T. Phillips and retired Coast Guard commandant James M. Loy).

Beyond simply defining leadership, there are many existential arguments about its nature. For example, there is no universal agreement as to whether leadership can be characterized as an art or as a science, although many agree to the compromise that it is a blend of both. There is the more serious problem of whether leadership is genetically acquired or can be learned, a variation on the "nature versus nurture" conundrum that vexes other disciplines like psychology and sociology. This debate is often ended quickly when it is realized that there is no point of further discussion if one accepts the "nature" side of the argument, whereas there is much to deliberate if the alternative is given legitimacy. And there are countless debates as to the relationship between leadership and personnel management, with those on one end of the scale proclaiming the two as virtually synonymous and those on the other end of the spectrum declaring that management is a business term and has no place in a military organization. And, of course, there are many variations in between. These and other questions make the study of leadership endlessly challenging, sometimes frustrating, but always worth the endeavor.

Approaches to leadership vary widely. So-called laundry lists of desirable attributes abound, as do metaphorical constructs such as the aforementioned Phillips and Loy book, which compares leadership to architectural components. Case-studies are a common method of exhibiting leadership practices (both good and bad), and there is the more recent proclivity for the "model" method, which prescribes the emulation of famous persons, such as Abraham Lincoln and Winston Churchill, as the key to successful leadership. Many attempts have been made to devise laws or principles (such as "praise in public, reprimand in private" or "do not micromanage"), some offering a few generic guides, others providing lengthy and detailed checklists.

There is a temptation to be discouraged by the diversity of these approaches, to wonder if perhaps there are no right answers nor any truly useful approaches. But the absence of absolutes does not diminish the relevance of the quest. The variety of methodologies and philosophies merely serves to emphasize the importance of the subject and to acknowledge its relativity, making the search for appropriate ways and means all the more intriguing.

Individuals

Whether formally assigned or naturally occurring, whether leading or being led, leadership is something we encounter in most walks of life, often beginning on the playground and continuing in various forms throughout our lives. It is no secret that there are rewards that come with being a leader, that it is often a badge of honor, an acceptable way for individuals in this democracy we so rightfully cherish to legitimately stand out from their peers.

But, like many worthwhile quests, it is also one fraught with great danger. The pages of *Navy Times* are all too frequently peppered with stories containing the words "relieved for cause," sad revelations of failure that are most often attributable—directly or peripherally—to problems in leadership. Sometimes those problems are perceived as epidemic in nature and the Navy prescribes a fleet-wide "stand down" or a new educational program as a cure. But more often than not, the problem lies with an individual, and for them there is no cure—it is too late to save their professional reputation and/or their careers. Individuals must rely on "preventive medicine" rather than an after-the-fact remedy, and that can only be obtained through healthy doses of common sense supplemented by a quest for self-edification.

It is naïve not to acknowledge that there are individuals who suffer from some character flaw that prevents them from ever becoming effective leaders, but it seems rather certain that most people have the means within them to become good leaders. It is also important to recognize that because people are very different, the process of self-edification does not reveal a clear-cut path to achievement. In the end, the process leads to a *style* of leadership that reflects the personality of the individual and other influences—including the self-edification process itself.

Full Disclosure

The desire for self-edification came early to me. As a young Navy petty officer, and later as a neophyte officer, I gratefully accepted the honor of being trusted with the authority to lead others. But that honor was accompanied by no small degree of trepidation as I quickly realized how much responsibility came with that authority. I desperately looked for guidance on how to lead well. I relied on active mentors, passively observed others practicing leadership, and read books and articles on the subject. And it should come as no surprise that many of the things I read in my quest to be a good leader came from the U.S. Naval Institute.

Besides being a member of the Naval Institute since first learning about it from Noah, I am now a member of the staff and have been for many years. I make no claim to objectivity, but I also have no doubt that my favorable bias for this organization is well-founded and defensible. For well over a century the Naval Institute has been serving the Navy by mentoring naval professionals, preserving sea service heritage, and providing a forum for constructive debate. From the earliest days of *Proceedings* magazine and through many books like *The Division Officer's Guide* and *Leadership Embodied,* actual and would-be leaders have participated in a dialogue that has kept the quest for better leadership alive and thriving.

Catalysts

Given the importance of the subject and the availability of so much relevant material, it was an easy decision to include leadership as one of the very first professional anthologies we have chosen to call "Wheel Books." Much more difficult has been the task of selecting what to include and what not. We could easily have created several anthologies on this subject and still have not scratched the surface.

What follows are the articles and excerpts that we did select for this one volume. Represented here is a small but potent slice of the larger corpus that resides in the rich Naval Institute archive. These selected pieces will not end the quest nor quell the debates, nor should they. But by offering insights that both edify and stimulate further thought and discussion, they serve as catalysts that will assist individuals who are in search of their own style of leadership.

Each of the selections that follow is believed to have "stand-alone" value, but their greatest worth is realized when viewed collectively. Readers can "cherry-pick" among the proffered pieces and be rewarded with nuggets of wisdom, or they may read this collection as a whole and benefit from the multifaceted blend of experience and cerebral exercise that it represents. When compared, some of these selections will seem virtual antitheses, offering up a healthy dialectic that will serve the appetites of those who hunger for food for thought. Others align more closely and may even appear as redundancies, but it is arguable that this repetition serves as reinforcement of meaningful ideas and, upon closer examination, the reader will find subtle differences worthy of consideration.

A by-product of this examination is the realization that we are indeed blessed with amazing military personnel who bring much more to their respective services than just seamanship, marksmanship, and the like. There is sapience in these pages that is remarkable, inspiring, and ultimately reassuring. I, for one, sleep better at night knowing that such impressive individuals have been and continue to be on watch.

As a whole, this collection not only provides guidance for actual and aspiring leaders but also serves as a testament to the importance of the subject to the naval profession. Leadership is a vital component of the everyday routine that makes military organizations functional, an indispensable ingredient to the extraordinary discipline that is required in times of crisis, and, ultimately, an essential catalyst to victory.

1 "LEADERSHIP FOR YOUNG OFFICERS AT SEA"

(Selection from chapter 1 of *Saltwater Leadership*)

RADM Robert O. Wray Jr., USN

Although Admiral Wray's recent book is meant primarily for junior sea-going officers, his first chapter is universal in its application and is an excellent starting point for a study of leadership. He sets the stage for further discussion by a straightforward, simple rendition of some of the ideas and questions that are addressed in many of the articles that follow. His tone is that of a cheerleader and is designed to encourage the reader while providing an introduction to some of the basics. This chapter sets the stage for the rest of the book, which primarily explores the work of others, providing a compendium of many of the approaches to leadership and charting a course through the complex world of leadership theory and practice.

"LEADERSHIP FOR YOUNG OFFICERS AT SEA"

(Selection from chapter 1 of *Saltwater Leadership: A Primer on Leadership for the Junior Sea-Service Officer*) by RADM Robert O. Wray Jr., USN (Naval Institute Press, 2013): 3–10.

This chapter does four things to get you started. It

- gives you the bottom line up front on leadership,
- answers the six basic questions on leadership,
- describes some basic models we can use to describe leadership, and
- explains how this book is organized and where we'll go from here.

So let's get started!

The Bottom Line, Up Front

This is the bottom line, right here on the first page:

Leadership matters. Everything in the world happens because of leadership.

Leadership is definable. It's not some hocus-pocus touchy-feely amorphous state of mind or relationship. It can be described and defined. It can be measured.

You can be a leader. It's learnable. You don't have to be born with it. Whatever you are today, you can become a leader, if you choose.

You, too, can make things happen.

Winston Churchill said, in writing to young officers like you: "Come on now all you young people all over the world. You have not an hour to lose. You must take your place in Life's fighting line. Twenty to twenty five! Those are the years. Don't be content with things as they are. Don't take No for an answer. Never submit to failure. You will make all kinds of mistakes; but as long as you are generous and true and also fierce, you cannot hurt the world!"

Are you ready to make things happen? Are you ready to be generous and true and fierce?

Are you ready to be a leader at sea?

You can be. Read this book!

The Six Basic Questions

"What is leadership, anyway?"

A good question. One that many people have studied for many years. There are a hundred definitions.

Webster's defines leadership as "the act of being a leader" and defines a leader as a person "with commanding authority or influence."

According to Navy General Order 21 (as first issued), leadership is defined as "the art of accomplishing the Navy's mission through people."

In the Commandant Instruction on leadership, the Coast Guard says leadership is "the ability to influence others to obtain their obedience, respect, confidence, and loyal cooperation."

The Army says that leadership is "influencing people—by providing purpose, direction, and motivation—while operating to accomplish the mission and improving the organization."

In my midshipman leadership text written several decades ago, leadership was somewhat loftily defined as "the art, science, or gift by which a person is enabled and privileged to direct the thoughts, plans, and actions of others in such a manner as to obtain and command their obedience, their confidence, their respect, and their loyal cooperation."

Field Marshal Bernard Montgomery said, "Leadership is the capacity and will to rally men and women to a common purpose and the character which inspires confidence." Similarly, Dwight Eisenhower said, "Leadership is the art of getting someone else to do something you want done because he wants to do it." Finally, Harry Truman echoed Eisenhower almost word for word when he said, "A leader is a man who has the ability to get other people to do what they don't want to do, and like it."

In other words: Leadership is the *process* of getting *people* to *do* things.

Now that might seem manipulative, crass, simplistic. Maybe it is. But in the end, things happen only because people make them happen, and someone has to get those people to make them happen. That's where leadership comes in.

"What's the difference between leadership and management?"

Another good question, and one often asked by junior officers. Like anything having to do with leadership, there are plenty of different answers. Some say that leadership is deciding *what* to do, and *why*, while management focuses on *how*.

Some say leadership focuses on accomplishing the mission, while management is about doing it efficiently.

Management author Ken Adelman says, "A leader knows what's best to do; a manager knows how best to do it."

Some say that leadership is about influencing, while management is more about operating. But notice that the Army definition of leadership cited previously includes both influencing and operating.

Renowned Harvard professor and leadership expert John Kotter says that management is about running things in steady state, while leadership is about causing change.

Management guru Warren Bennis laid out the following distinctions between the two:

- Leaders do the right things; managers do things right.
- Leaders innovate; managers administer.
- Leaders inspire; managers control.
- Leaders think long-term; managers think short-term.
- Leaders originate; managers imitate.
- Leaders challenge the status quo; managers accept the status quo.

As usual, all these views are right, in their own way. For the junior officer, you will be providing both management and leadership to the folks who work for you, and often the two will overlap. For instance, say you're working on a tough project and one of your key people has a family situation that needs attention. Deciding to let him go tend to his family, even if it hurts your team strength, is a leadership decision. Figuring out how to adjust other team schedules to make it work is more about management.

"Why is leadership important?"

In the world of the junior officer at sea, does leadership really matter? Isn't it really about standing a good watch and managing the few people that might work for you?

Leadership is important to you in two ways.

First, it will help you do your job better, today. You are not in charge of three bookkeepers in office cubicles, working nine-to-five weekdays. Management alone could probably get that job done.

Rather, you are responsible for far more people, under far more arduous, difficult, and unpredictable circumstances. You and your ship are working 24/7, year-round, in bad weather, in difficult situations, in conflict, sometimes under adversity, or even under fire. These conditions call for more than management. Your decisions can place your people into danger. Sending a mariner topside at night in freezing foul weather to find and fix a thorny problem isn't management—it takes leadership to have influence like that. Leading a team into a smoke-filled space to put out a fire isn't management; it's leadership, pure and simple.

Being a leader is critical to get your job done, even as the most junior officer on your ship. If you need further evidence, look at your performance evaluation. Is there a block for "management"? Probably not. Is there a block to evaluate you in leadership? Absolutely.

Second, leadership is important to you today because in most cases, it is the coin of the realm for your advancement in the sea services. The path to the top is built of critical leadership steps, without which you'll never progress. Whether your goal is to become a master or chief engineer of a ship, or a captain in the Coast Guard or Navy, you can't do it without successfully demonstrating leadership at every level as you progress.

"Is leadership innate or learned?"

It's 3 percent innate and 97 percent learned.

Those numbers aren't exact, obviously—they're my view, and as you'll find in leadership study, everyone has a different point of view. But based on my forty years of leadership experience and study, they're pretty close.

Some inherited traits are helpful. For instance, it helps if you're tall. The overwhelming majority of presidential elections have been won by the taller candidate. In the corporate marketplace, taller people, overall, get paid slightly more, and are promoted slightly more often. Statistically, physical attractiveness is similarly rewarded.

It also helps if you're intelligent. Intelligence can help you to be a better communicator, a better solver of problems. It helps you to learn leadership skills faster. There is a positive correlation between intelligence and advancement in corporate management hierarchies. In other words, senior managers, in general, score higher in intelligence tests than middle managers. Similarly, chief executives are, in general, measurably smarter than senior managers.

Finally, for some circumstances, it helps if you're big and strong. In some groups, size and strength can assist in leadership. In other groups, it's immaterial.

But that's about it. All the other leadership traits—character, speaking ability, empathy, organization, vision, honesty, work ethic, amiability, courage, perseverance—are all acquired. They are all learned. They are all available to you. If you didn't get them growing up, you can get them now, if you choose.

"How does one become a leader?"

If you wanted to play the piano, what would you do? Most likely, you would:

- study a book on music and theory
- get a teacher to give you lessons
- practice the piano
- watch and listen to others play

If you want to learn French, if you want to become a chef, if you want to hit a curveball, if you want to learn virtually anything, it might include:

- study
- a teacher
- practice
- observation of others

So it is with leadership. Leadership can be learned using these four basic tenets.

COL Art Athens, a leadership professor at the Naval Academy and former commandant of the Merchant Marine Academy at Kings Point, has written in his book *Preparing to Lead* that leadership can be learned through six fundamental building blocks:

1. self-knowledge
2. observation
3. intellectual base
4. mentoring
5. adversity
6. experience

His six building blocks are nouns—they are results that provide the foundation of leadership. My four items above—studying, getting taught, practicing, and observing—are verbs. They are what you, the young officer at sea, can *do* to acquire those six building blocks.

Remember, you can become a leader. You can learn. You do it by:

- studying leadership
- having a mentor or a teacher who can help you perfect your skills
- practicing and experiencing leadership
- watching other leaders around you, both good and bad

SPOM: Study, Practice, Observe, Mentor. It's not rocket science. But, by the way, if you wanted to learn rocket science, you'd learn it the same way!

One note: the four steps above all require one thing: *will*. You have to *want* to be a leader. You don't become one through osmosis or through mere wishful thinking. You can wish you were a great piano player, but unless you take the steps to make it happen, it won't happen. ADM William Pratt, former chief of Naval Operations, said, "Few realize that the growth to sound leadership is a life's work. Ambition alone will not encompass it. [It] is a long, hard road to travel."

Editor's Note

The sixth question mentioned previously relates to the reason for and structure of the book itself and is, therefore, omitted for this anthology.

2 "LEADERSHIP: THE THEORY BEHIND THE PRINCIPLES"

Maj Thomas U. Wall, USMC

The quest for a better understanding of leadership is by no means exclusive to the armed services. Business and academia, in particular, share that pursuit, and in this article Major Wall acknowledges some of those ventures and contends that the military should be "open and receptive to input from all *reasonable* sources." He explores some of the more prominent thinking on the subject, including the fairly well-known works of Douglas McGregor ("Theory X and Theory Y") and Abraham Maslow ("hierarchy of needs"), with an eye toward adapting such thinking to the special needs of the military—the Marine Corps officer in particular—whom he interestingly, and somewhat provocatively, describes as "a manager of violence."

"LEADERSHIP: THE THEORY BEHIND THE PRINCIPLES"

By Maj Thomas U. Wall, USMC, U.S. Naval Institute *Proceedings* (December 1976): 72–77.

The Marine Corps' approach to leadership has been based upon two precepts: (1) a great respect for and confidence in the competence of fellow Marines, and

(2) decisive and aggressive action to guarantee mission accomplishment. The Marine Corps leader is, quite simply, a manager of violence.

My concern is with describing, investigating, and analyzing our approach to leadership with respect to theory and current research. Where are we? And perhaps more importantly, where are we going?

Traditionally, investigations of leadership in the military have attempted to explain the leader by analyzing those individual traits or leadership principles which are believed to represent effective leadership. The theory has been that if we can select, train, and commission individuals who have demonstrated academic ability (by earning a college degree) and motivation (by completing a rigorous pre-commissioning training cycle), we can teach them the traits and principles of leadership which will enable them to be effective leaders in a combat situation. This theory is based upon several critical assumptions: (1) that leadership skills considered "effective" can be identified and isolated; (2) that there is a military environment requiring a specific leadership approach; and (3) that the indoctrination and training cycle presently used encourages the teaching of leadership skills which will improve leader effectiveness.

I will address these three assumptions by discussing: (1) some characteristics of leadership; (2) the military environment; (3) some thoughts about attitudes, values, and motivation; (4) leadership training as it currently exists in the Marine Corps; and (5) some examples of behavioral/motivational information which can be incorporated in the training cycle to increase its long-term effectiveness. Following the summary, I will address some problems and future directions I hope that our leadership training program will take in order to increase our understanding of the leader and his (or her) special talents.

Contemporary researchers have described leadership in terms of virtually every conceivable variable. Ralph M. Stogdill's *Handbook of Leadership* reviews the literature quite comprehensibly. Leadership effectiveness seems to be controlled by three factors: the individual, the group, and the situation. From the individual Marine's point of view, the leader's two most important functions involve: (1) the initiation of group structure, and (2) consideration for individual needs. In other words, the superior or subordinate judges a leader's effectiveness based upon the degree to which the leader satisfies the individual's needs and the needs (mission) of the organization.

Leadership style, quite simply, reflects the personality of the leader. Hundreds of styles have been identified and lumped into categories which describe leader behavior. Researcher sophistication appears to be a function of the number and complexity of leader categories—allow me to expose my complete lack of sophistication by contending that, for the purposes of this essay, all leaders can be judged on their ability to satisfy needs. If we establish a continuum between task orientation and people orientation, all leaders will fall somewhere between the two. Task-oriented leaders concern themselves with only the mission, autocratically making decisions and allowing little room for individual initiative or action. The group-oriented leader encourages democratic participation in decision making, is concerned with member interaction and satisfaction, and provides for low group structure and little supervision.

In the eyes of superiors and subordinates, leader orientation is a direct determinant of leader effectiveness. Situations will arise which require the leader to emphasize either task or people orientation. If, however, the satisfaction of both individual and organizational needs is the key to effective leadership, the leader's innate style must register somewhere in the middle of the people-task continuum, recognizing that both people and organizational needs require satisfaction, and appreciating when, why, and how to shift the emphasis from one to the other.

I have said that effective leaders satisfy the needs of their superiors and subordinates and those of the organization. However, satisfaction of the individual's needs is not synonymous with accomplishment of the mission. Complete need satisfaction is not only impossible, it is undesirable. The presence of unsatisfied needs is a prerequisite for motivation. The objective is to treat each person in accordance with his needs. By recognizing and dealing with these people needs, the stage is set for the leader to monitor the intrinsic or extrinsic motivation required and to ensure that action is channeled in accordance with the goals and priorities of the organization.

There are three factors which allow for the emergence of the Marine Corps leader. Our recruiting program stresses leadership as the primary role and responsibility of the potential officer or staff NCO. Motivation to fulfill this role is largely responsible for application. Personality or style allows the individual to surface and be recognized among his peers. Ability—physical fitness, intelligence, organizing expertise, etc.—establishes power in one or more areas by virtue of demonstrated competence.

Once an individual's application to join the organization has been accepted, leadership evaluation begins. An individual either falls by the wayside or moves up through the chain of command based upon his ability to maintain the delicate balance between his own motivation, personality, ability, situation, and luck. On the average, individual factors in combination with organizational factors either establish effectiveness (promotion) or document ineffectiveness (nonselection for promotion).

Typical of the overgeneralized misrepresentation of the military leader by some academicians who have little experience with Marine Corps leadership is the following quote from F. G. Fiedler's 1969 *Psychology Today* article. "Frequently advocated in conventional supervisory and military systems . . . the authoritarian, task-oriented leader takes all responsibility for making decisions and directing the group members. His rationale is simple: I do the thinking and you carry out the orders." Is there a military environment which can be isolated in theoretical discussions of organizations?

I have thus far alluded to the existence of organization and people needs without discussing them. People needs include:

- Understanding one's role
- Liking one's role
- Receiving appropriate rewards (in whatever form) commensurate with investment
- Trusting other organizational members
- Feeling a valuable part of the organization

Organizational needs include:

- Resources (people, bullets, beans, etc.)
- Production (the input, throughput, and output associated with training Marines for combat)
- Distribution (providing reliable combat power, providing manpower for public service projects, etc.)
- Healthy public relations
- Adaptability to change (in mission, strength, resources, etc.)
- Internal and external coordination (the essential function of the leader)

Any organization which provides a service depends upon the fulfillment of these needs, both people and organizational, in order to exist, regardless of its peculiar mission. Non-satisfaction of the individual's needs usually results in rebellion, quitting, or attempts to bring about change. Mission accomplishment is the ultimate casualty when organizational needs are not met.

Theoretically, the Marine Corps is no different than any organization of its size and complexity in terms of these needs. In practice, however, the military leader makes several unique commitments which separate his organization from more traditional organizational discussions and which go hand-in-hand with acceptance of the leadership role. These include: (1) the understanding that he is being hired and evaluated primarily as a leader, regardless of any other contributions made to the organization; (2) the recognition that the organization's primary goal is proficiency in combat; and (3) the realization that through external civilian control, the employment of combat skills may be in conflict with personal, ethical, social, or moral values. The full impact of these commitments becomes clear only when push comes to shove.

The Marine Corps has as much potential for success or failure as any other organization. Leaders must function to see that needs, both personal and organizational, are met. The failure to recognize and understand these needs adds to the difficulty in completing the mission.

Attitudes are dispositions each of us formulate to provide a frame of reference for the formation of opinions. An attitude may be based upon either emotion or fact. An unfavorable attitude toward the military, for example, will support negative opinions concerning the value of the Marine Corps. According to N.R.F. Maier, attitudes determine meaning, reconcile contradictions between conflicting opinions, and select and organize facts. Attitudes, even when confronted with conflicting facts, are sometimes difficult to change.

The formation of attitudes is a natural result of experience. The leader may have little or no control over attitude formation, depending upon the situation and the group, but he must be attuned to the fact that attitudes may provide support for or resistance to the accomplishment of the mission. The leader's job becomes one of stimulating positive attitude formation. The first step in this process is to recognize individual differences and to foster honest and constructive communication—both vertically and horizontally—within the organization.

Values are concerned with the nature of man. They are personal commitments which are basic to action (i.e., freedom, education, despotism, etc.). Douglas McGregor has outlined two theories dealing with two extreme approaches we may take when interacting with others. One's attitude, stemming from one's personal value system, toward superiors and subordinates helps to determine which approach or combination thereof we choose.

Theory X maintains that: (1) the average human being has an inherent dislike of work and will avoid it if he can; (2) most people must be coerced, controlled, directed, and threatened with punishment to get them to put forth adequate effort toward the achievement of organizational objectives; and (3) the average human being prefers to be directed, wishes to avoid responsibility, has relatively little ambition, and wants security above all.

Theory Y contends that: (1) work is as natural as play or rest; (2) man will exercise self-direction and self-control in the service of objectives to which he is committed; (3) commitment to objectives is a function of the rewards associated with their achievement; (4) the average human being learns not only to accept but to seek responsibility; (5) imagination, ingenuity, and creativity are widely distributed in the population; and (6) the intellectual potential of the average human is only partially utilized.

McGregor believes that these theories represent assumptions which we make about others, and that they determine our approach to superiors and subordinates. The leadership activity stemming from a Theory X approach is direction and control. A Theory Y approach assumes that others are mature, ambitious, creative, willing to learn, and seek responsibility.

To say that all individuals can be treated from a Theory Y perspective is naive and dangerous. There are situations which, and people who, require a Theory X approach. In an organization whose mission demands aggressive action, commitment, and dedication, the leader who blindly assumes that his command is brave, honest, and true may find out differently as he alone crosses the line of departure. The foundation for a Theory Y approach is not a "gut" level belief in the goodness of man. The foundation stems from the fact that the effective leader has a complete and honest appreciation for the capabilities and limitations of his people. He knows their needs and problems, based upon one-to-one interaction and close personal observation. He has measured objectively their performance in realistic training situations. He has developed a unit spirit and fostered a cooperative atmosphere. He has set the example. He has participated, giving more of himself than he has expected of them.

The effective leader in fact *assumes* nothing in dealing with people. Rather, he knows that mission accomplishment is achieved through people. A thorough understanding of his people allows him to help them satisfy their needs while utilizing their talents in directing their efforts toward the accomplishment of the mission.

Motivation is based upon the satisfaction of needs arranged in a hierarchy, according to Abraham Maslow. As one need is met, another appears in its place. Man works to satisfy his never-ending needs.

Man's most basic needs are physiological—food, shelter, warmth, etc. Once a need is satisfied, it ceases to be a motivator of behavior. Needs on this first level are short-term and readily identifiable, but they must be met before the next level of needs become motivators.

Safety needs—protection from danger, threat, etc.—are on the next level. The needs are not for the total absence of dangers and threats, but rather for the chance of an even break. When confident of a fair chance of success, the individual is willing to take risks.

The next level of needs requiring satisfaction are the social needs—belonging, association, acceptance, giving and receiving friendship, and love. It generally is assumed by ineffective leaders that these needs threaten the needs of the organization. Instead, they serve to foster team spirit and cohesive action. When they are not met, they encourage resistance, antagonism, and uncooperative attitude formation.

Beyond the social needs are the ones of the greatest significance and importance to the leader and his people—the egoistic needs. They are of two kinds: (1) the need for self-respect and self-confidence; and (2) the need for status, recognition, and appreciation. Unlike the lower-level needs, they are rarely satisfied.

On the top rung of the hierarchy are the needs for self-actualization—the realization of one's potential and continued self-development. Although the most difficult to satisfy, these needs can be recognized through the promotion of education and the delegation of leadership responsibility to the lowest level of a unit's chain of command.

Maslow's theory provides operational definitions of the people needs which must be satisfied within organizations. McGregor's theories outline the two extremes in approaching superiors and subordinates.

Opinions are derived from attitudes which stem from one's values. The leader can influence all three either positively or negatively, depending upon his relationship to and understanding of his superiors and subordinates. A sincerely positive attitude displayed by subordinates can be an indication of leader effectiveness. A negative attitude toward the job, fellow Marines, or the organization is an indication of poor leadership.

The leader's job, then, is: (1) to help create an atmosphere which encourages the formation of positive attitudes by approaching subordinates in a mature and understanding fashion, and (2) to recognize and capitalize on the inherent motivation required by individuals in satisfying their own needs. Accomplishing these objectives requires a thorough knowledge of subordinates and an appreciation for the individual factors which motivate people to act.

Can an individual be trained to become a leader? What basic qualities must he possess prior to undergoing training so as to enhance success? Can leadership abilities demonstrated in one situation be effective in another?

I have discussed some pertinent behavioral theories and presented an operational definition of leadership within the Marine Corps. The question of leadership training has been given extensive attention over the years. Stogdill reports the results of numerous studies which seem to indicate that: (1) leadership is transferable from one situation to another, depending upon the nature of the tasks required; (2) leadership in high school and college *tends* to be predictive of leadership in adult life; (3) research on leadership is generally inadequate in both design and execution to answer the crucial questions such as the effectiveness of training on group performance; and (4) the best predictor of future leadership success is past success in similar situations.

These findings provide support for the contention that identified effective leaders have the potential to transfer leadership skills among similar situations. Effective leaders in high school and college can be identified. The problem arises when we assume that their leadership skills are transferable from the campus to combat. We currently have no consistently effective predictor of success; but, recognizing the *potential* for transferability as demonstrated by Stogdill, it seems appropriate to recruit leaders from high schools and colleges.

Currently, leadership training is structured to: (1) measure and reward task accomplishment, and (2) force-feed leadership principles and traits. The prospective leader is first evaluated on his ability to get things done. Little emphasis is placed on measuring his skill in dealing with people. We assume that if he gets the job done, he has satisfied the individual needs of his superiors and subordinates, but this is too often not the case. Candidates can be tested in physical fitness, general military subjects, tactics, drill, and weapons. Future leaders can be evaluated on their ability to muster their people on time, complete a day compass march, or disassemble a weapon. It often seems inappropriate to *waste* the limited time and resources available in teaching interpersonal skills.

We stress leadership principles and traits in an effort to force-feed individual behaviors which have proven successful in the past. The application of principles depends primarily upon the individual's personality and the situation in which he finds himself. As a general rule they provide an excellent framework, but a general understanding of behavior and motivation is necessary in order to effectively apply these principles, assuming they are even in keeping with the personal leadership style of the leader. Measuring task accomplishment and teaching principles certainly has its place in the program. In addition, however, leadership training should be structured to measure the people and task orientations of the candidate, officer, or NCO, and to teach: (1) the interpersonal skills which will aid in recognizing and dealing with individual needs, and (2) the motivational and behavior skills which must be employed to accomplish the mission.

What behavioral and motivational skills need to be taught to the prospective leader? How will these skills help him to deal with people?

A comprehensive treatise of effective leadership skills is beyond the scope of this particular essay; however, I want to discuss power and delegation of authority, two topics which could and should be incorporated in leadership training to supplement the teaching of principles.

Power, for the purposes of this discussion, is defined in terms of the influence that the leader can exert on the superior or the subordinate. Five bases or sources of power identified by J. R. P. French and B. Raven are: (1) reward power, based upon the leader's ability to provide rewards; (2) coercive power, based upon the expectation that the leader will punish those who fail to act according to his influence; (3) legitimate power, based upon the organizational norm that seniority or rank provides power; (4) referent power, based upon personal attraction for, respect for, or a desire to identify with the leader because of his perceived competence; and (5) expert power, based upon the leader's special knowledge or talent in one or more areas.

The relationship between the leader, his basis of power, and the group is quite complex. French and Raven have hypothesized the following: (1) for all five types, the stronger the basis of power, the greater the power; (2) in general, referent power will have the broadest range; (3) any attempt to utilize power outside one's range will tend to reduce one's power; and (4) coercion results in decreased attraction for the leader and resistance; reward power results in increased attraction and low resistance.

With respect to these sources of power, Stogdill has found: (1) perceived expertness tends to legitimize the leadership role; (2) being liked and accepted by the group gives the leader more influence than if he is not liked or accepted; (3) a group member is better able to resist coercive power when he has an opportunity to interact with peers or to observe other members who disobey; (4) group members become more passive and dependent in ambiguous situations than in clearly defined power situations; and (5) failure to provide role and task definitions tends to result in member dissatisfaction, resistance to the leader, and disruption of group activities.

Recognizing one's base of power allows for a greater understanding of one's capabilities and limitations when dealing with others. Referent power may result from setting the example. The implications for the leader are important. A theoretical understanding of the concept of power and authority provides background information which is necessary for the effective application of proven leadership principles.

Another, sometimes troublesome, responsibility for the leader involves the delegation of authority. Too often we find it easier to do the job ourselves. Many leaders who have established themselves by virtue of their ability to get the job done find it difficult to allow subordinates the freedom of action necessary to plan, do, and control tasks. This is particularly true of those new to the formal leadership role. Leaders see their jobs as ones of planning and controlling, while attempting to delegate the "doing." Subordinates, assigned a task with no say in its planning or control, become frustrated and feel restricted or oversupervised. Under such conditions they often do poor jobs, which reinforces the leader's belief that he should have done the job himself and fosters a Theory X approach toward the subordinates.

It is important to remember that subordinates, although requiring role structure, need also to exercise their planning and controlling skills. The lesson for the leader to remember is that subordinates normally seek responsibility; and, in allowing them to grow and to develop within the organization, it is necessary to assign tasks without necessarily explaining how they are to be done.

The preceding examples are the types of behavioral and motivational material which can be included in the leadership training cycle to supplement the guidelines provided by the principles. A foundation in behavioral and motivational science is a requirement of no less importance for the effective leader than the measurement of his skills in completing tasks.

In my opinion: (1) leadership skills considered effective can be identified and isolated, but further research into their processes is required; (2) on a practical level, perhaps, there is a military environment, but the leader's approach to his role is as dynamic as the range of individual personalities is broad; and (3) our present leadership training program needs expansion to include the theory behind the proven principles and traits which are now being taught.

The Marine Corps' ability to get the job done is basic to the organization. Mission accomplishment, in a sense, is taken for granted. Its organization, orientation, training, and structure are geared toward this end. Can an organization which places such a premium on the mission afford to neglect the needs of its people? I think not. The effective Marine Corps leader, in fact, prides himself on a realistic appreciation of human needs based upon a thorough knowledge of subordinates. This approach to leadership has theoretical as well as practical support. Our leadership principles advocate a Theory Y approach to the individual, stress participation in decision-making, and recognize the hierarchy of human needs.

Motivation to accept leadership responsibility, a personality and the situational opportunity which allows the individual to surface, and the specific abilities which ensure the acquisition of broad-based power and the demonstration of competence all provide the potential leader with a leadership role. Very practically, leadership effectiveness is based upon performance. Once in the role, the leader sinks or swims based upon his or her ability to satisfy needs and to motivate performance. Training can be effective with the right person in the right group at the right time. Military leaders make somewhat unique commitments, but the organization does not significantly differ, in terms of problems and expectations, than other groups of its size and complexity. The military establishment is a powerful and influential force with the potential to preserve or to destroy our civilization. It seems to me that the direction in which this force moves will be dramatically determined by the effectiveness of its civilian managers and organizational leaders.

Leadership as a phenomenon is currently developing within the academic community into a highly sophisticated area of social science research. Much data is being collected which may lead to interesting and perhaps revolutionary changes in the process of selecting and training leaders. It is in the interest of ensuring that the Marine Corps leader is exposed to and perhaps incorporates some of this information in his bag of leadership tricks that I have written this paper. For the same reasons I believe that it is important to highlight some of the problems with our current leadership approach:

- There is too much emphasis on task accomplishment without a corresponding effort to measure and teach the interpersonal skills necessary for dealing with the needs of the superiors and the subordinates.
- There is no empirical measurement of current leadership effectiveness with regard to the leader's people or mission orientation. This information could tell us where we stand and in which areas we may wish to make some changes in our training programs.
- There is no attempt to determine the people or mission orientation of individuals before they assume the leadership role. Capitalizing on strengths and attacking weaknesses in leadership training will increase training effectiveness.
- Too often a Theory X approach to subordinates is coupled with a Theory Y approach to superiors.
- There is a tendency to teach leadership in a vacuum without looking at the leader with relation to the group he will lead.

These problems have practical solutions. I am currently attempting a pilot study which I hope will lead to a practical way of measuring the people and task orientations of our current and future Marine Corps leaders. Behavioral, motivational, and interpersonal training can be incorporated in the training cycle. This training will broaden the scope of our approach, provide some theoretical support for our practical knowledge, and give the Marine Corps leader a greater understanding of why he does his job as effectively, or perhaps as ineffectively, as he does.

Lest my brothers in green falsely accuse me of being a softhearted sentimentalist who wants to make everyone in the Marine Corps *feel* good by preaching more human relations and less discipline, let me set the record straight. The approach to leadership which I advocate is not one of permissiveness—it is one of increased sophistication. It is not enough to emulate principles or to complete tasks. It is necessary to understand, motivate, and control.

Most Marines, myself included, pride themselves on their understanding of and devotion to their leadership responsibilities. The Marine Corps' leadership training program is both theoretically and pragmatically based; it has proven itself on the battlefield as well as in the classroom. My concern is that we, as leaders in this organization, recognize the tremendous interest and effort being devoted to leadership in the business and educational communities, and that we remain open and receptive to input from all *reasonable* sources. We leaders have an enormous responsibility in ensuring that our unique missions are accomplished as required; but I see an even greater responsibility to our superiors and subordinates to ensure that in the area of leadership, they receive the most effective that science, industry, and experience can provide.

3 "THE PROFESSION OF LEADING"

CAPT David Tyler, USN

Since its founding, the Naval Institute has imparted information through the traditional means of magazine articles and books. Through the years, additional means have been employed to carry the Institute's missions, such as oral histories and seminars. And most recently, modern technology has provided additional weapons to the arsenal, such as websites, social media, and blogs. Captain David Tyler has made good use of the latter by posting a series titled "Perspectives on Military Leadership." In the brief but compelling sample below, Captain Tyler addresses several aspects of leadership, ending with a call for continuing study—which is the very reason this Wheel Book was created—to reinforce enduring principles while embracing the ever-burgeoning body of knowledge we are confronted with in this age of information.

"THE PROFESSION OF LEADING"

By CAPT David Tyler, USN, U.S. Naval Institute blog (March 2014).

For military professionals, leading is not a collateral activity; it is a full-time, continuous responsibility. To be effective in any field of endeavor one must first know how to use the tools of the trade. While knowing the subject of one's profession can be gained through study and experience, unless that knowledge rests in the forefront of one's consciousness, where it serves as a backdrop for influencing daily activities, it will be as useless as an unread book.

Leadership is about convincing others to act in a desired way. Hence, the art of the profession lies in persuading others that it is in their best interest to pursue a particular objective. Convincing, then, is what distinguishes leadership from other methods that rely on compellence or coercion, such as dictatorships or subjugation, to achieve objectives.

Yet getting others to willingly work to achieve a desired end takes more than eloquent talk or irrefutable evidence. The willingness to follow is a pivotal emotional commitment taken by an individual. It is an emotional investment by one individual in another based on the belief that the leader is a credible individual with worthy ideals. The currency exchanged in a follower–leader contract is trust. Thus, to reap the benefits of effective leadership, mutual trust must be continuously nurtured and reinforced.

With information abundantly available, the primary challenge for most leaders is not a lack of knowledge but the ability to pierce the fog of daily distractions and actively apply ingrained leadership tenets.

Effective leaders are guided by prevailing winds of enduring principles but informed by present realities. They do this by continuously learning and refreshing their thoughts about leadership. Professional leaders must study the subject of leadership regularly in much the same way a medical professional continuously studies the tools of his trade.

4 "THE NAVAL OFFICER: MANAGER OR LEADER?"

LT R. T. E. Bowler III, USN, and LT D. R. Bowler, USN

Lieutenants R. T. E. and D. R. Bowler tackle the prickly problem of leadership versus management. This is a continuing source of discussion and debate that sometimes can be rather passionate. Behind the debate lurks the struggle between those who advocate a symbiosis between business and military leadership techniques, and those who insist that the two professions are too different to allow too much overlap. The Bowler brothers attempt to clarify the distinctions while acknowledging that "the management and leadership relationships in the two paradigms, though different, are not incompatible." In the end, they contend that it is essential for the naval officer to "crystallize in his mind the relationship between management and leadership," and that this "should be done at the expense of learning exotic new civilian management techniques."

"THE NAVAL OFFICER: MANAGER OR LEADER?"

By LT R. T. E. Bowler III, USN, and LT D. R. Bowler, USN, U.S. Naval Institute *Proceedings* (December 1975): 64–67.

Within the Navy today, two philosophical paradigms are competing. Each views the relationship between management and leadership differently and, because they do, they are planting the seeds for a potential identity crisis in the mind of the young naval officer caught between them. One, the management paradigm, asserts that the effective management of scarce resources within the command is the primary objective. Leadership in this model is considered only as an important element of the management process. The management paradigm is prevalent in the civilian establishment. The military establishment, conversely, adheres predominantly to the philosophy that leadership is the principal means to an end, citing the ability to manage as one of several secondary traits the successful leader exhibits. Is this difference in the relationship between management and leadership, as offered by the two paradigms, important to the naval officer of today? For the confused young officer who cannot answer the question, "Am I a manager or a leader first?" we think the difference is important. And for the middle-grade officer who finds himself working side by side with a civilian counterpart, an understanding of the difference between the two management/leadership relationships is also important.

Our purpose in this essay is not to provide a checklist whereby the manager can become a good leader or the leader a good manager. Rather we seek to aid the junior officer in recognizing the conflicting paradigms and their origins, to explain their differences and similarities, and to orient the individual officer in such a manner that he can successfully bridge the philosophical gap between management and leadership. In short, we are attempting to develop an acceptable internal consensus regarding the relationship between management and leadership for the Navy of today.

This management-versus-leadership incompatibility, which we have said lies at the foundation of our identity crisis, did not develop overnight. The necessity for strong and capable leadership has always been a hallmark of our service.

Leadership grasps the human element. In the evolution of our Navy, weapon systems have come and gone, but the sailor alone has remained. Indeed the sailor of the Seventies is a more socially aware, better-educated individual than his predecessor of even 20 to 30 years ago. This does not eliminate the need for leadership; rather, it strengthens the requirement and demands the naval leader of the Seventies be more sensitive as well as better educated than his predecessors. In any case, where one finds sailors behaving and thinking individually, the need exists for leadership to control and mold them into a combat-capable team. The leadership paradigm, in which men mean more than guns, then, is the traditional naval philosophy.

Challenging the leadership paradigm is that of management—by no means unimportant. Before World War II, management per se was not widely recognized as a distinct profession or calling. Management suffered then as a euphemism for "getting the job done." Since World War II, however, the near exponential technological advances have produced similar increases in the complexity of "getting the job done." This, in turn, has generated the need for skilled men whose sole function is to manage effectively. The growth in the field of scientific management alone demonstrates this need. Such disciplines as operations research, systems analysis, and computer systems management demand as managers bright young naval officers if our Navy hopes to keep abreast of the advancing technological wave.

As the Navy's demand for managers increases—while its relative training resources dwindle—the Navy cannot be expected to completely provide in-house facilities to develop its own managers. The solution is to capitalize on the management knowledge, gained at a civilian university or institution, of the incoming junior officer; or to interrupt the short career of the officer already in the service and either send him to a civilian school for a management-related degree or to a Navy school to be educated in civilian concepts of management. Because of resource restrictions, therefore, we find that the management techniques employed in the Navy are predominantly borrowed from the civilian sector. The end result is that the young naval manager and his civilian counterpart are often performing the same tasks, save for the "labels." Herein lies the crux of the identity crisis. Framed in the philosophy of the civilian management paradigm, the young naval manager is taught to emphasize the final two elements of the "men-money-materials" triad and to focus foremost on the goals of the organization. But from an omnipotent voice in the sky (the ghost of naval officers past?), he is admonished to, above all else, know and care for his men—to lead them.

Emphasis on management is not solely a civilian by-product. It stems from our own house too. Then–Secretary of the Navy, Fred Korth, in an August 1963 *Proceedings* article titled "The Challenge to Navy Management," wrote of his and his immediate subordinates' functions: "I *manage* the Department of the Navy; the Chief of Naval Operations and the Commandant of the Marine Corps *manage* their respective armed services [our italics] . . ." Throughout the article, virtually no mention is made of the leadership that is the putative hallmark of the naval service. Can anyone doubt, therefore, why the junior officer would genuinely pose the question, "Am I a manager or a leader first?"

Conflicting philosophies, conflicting requirements, and conflicting responsibilities confront the individual officer almost daily. If a naval officer is no more than a manager wearing shoulder boards, so be it, and let us say so. But if a naval officer, as a manager, is something unique, then let us say that. The young naval officer nearing the end of his term of obligated service, trying to make the crucial decision whether to stay in or depart the service, tends to wax philosophic and is especially vulnerable to such soul-searching questions. We believe this essay will help him answer this question.

To bring into focus the question of the relationship between management and leadership as it relates to the naval officer, we will consider in succession the management-leadership relationship in the civilian sector, the military relationship, a comparison and contrast between the peacetime military manager and his civilian counterpart, and, finally, a comparison and contrast between military and civilian managers in wartime.

In James J. Cribbin's *Effective Managerial Leadership* (New York: American Management Association, 1972), we find management defined as "the scientific art of attaining intended organizational objectives by working effectively with and through the human and material resources of the firm." Cribbin also proffers a lengthy definition of leadership, but we will present a military-oriented definition of leadership later. It is important to note in his discussion of management—and this is typical of many management texts—Cribbin clearly indicates that leadership is but *an element* of the overall management process. In other words, while the outstanding manager is most likely an effective leader, it does not necessarily follow that the effective leader is an outstanding manager. Thus we see that, according to the current civilian management philosophy, leadership is clearly subservient to managership. Again from Cribbin, "Management always has a strong element of the logical, the rational, the financial, the impersonal, the analytical, and the quantitative. Leadership, in contrast, always involves the chemistry that exists between the alpha fish and those he leads." For the young naval manager then, through his civilian-oriented management training, is told that leadership is secondary in importance to the "scientific art of attaining intended organizational objectives" because it is intangible, subjective, and nonmeasurable.

From the military establishment, we hear a different drummer. One of the most widely read professional books by junior naval officers, Captain John V. Noel's *Division Officer's Guide* (Sixth Edition, Annapolis, Maryland: Naval Institute Press, 1972), defines leadership (taken from General Order 21) as "the art of accomplishing the Navy's mission through people. It is the sum of those qualities of intellect, of human understanding, and of moral character that enable a man to inspire and to manage a group of people successfully. Effective leadership, therefore, is based on personal example, good management practices, and moral responsibility." Notice that in this military-oriented definition, at least, the function of managing is viewed as but one element of the overall leadership function. The civilian management paradigm would charge the military of putting the leadership cart before the management horse.

The difference in viewpoints is obvious. Civilian doctrine, in which many of our naval officers are schooled, emphasizes the management function, while military doctrine, which is taught to those same officers, emphasizes the leadership function. From this basic contradiction rises a fundamental question: why are they different? Is the military definition simply antiquated, a product of tradition that has fallen behind the times? (Certainly this would not be the first time the military has been accused of committing that particular sin.) Or is there a plausible reason why the Navy and the other armed services emphasize the leadership side of the coin? We maintain the latter to be true. The conflicting views of the management-leadership relationship, when placed in the proper context, are not incompatible for the naval officer who is asked to manage and to lead with energy and effectiveness. This compatibility can be understood by investigating the roles and functions of the civilian and military manager in peacetime and in wartime.

Since the naval officer may spend most or all of his career in a peacetime environment, it is natural to compare first the roles of the civilian and naval managers in peacetime. In comparing the naval manager with the civilian manager, and in later citing some differences, we emphasize that we are not denigrating either one. Each is indispensable to his respective organization.

In peacetime, whether the naval manager be ashore or afloat, many similarities exist between him and a civilian manager. Both are, in a broad sense, trying to use their scarce resources—men, money, and materials—in the most efficient manner possible to accomplish the goals of their respective organizations. Admittedly, the measures of performance are different. The civilian manager is first and foremost trying to maximize profits. His gauge of success is that which appears on the "bottom line." In the Navy, our benchmark is the elusive goal of "battle readiness." We have not managed effectively if we cannot put to sea a well-trained, well-supplied, combat-capable ship, squadron, or submarine. Nevertheless, the essence of the managing function in both environments is the same, that of getting the job done in the best possible manner, with the resources available. Is there a great difference between the destroyer commanding officer who attempts—with diminishing OpTars, continuing personnel shortages, and reduced operating time—to prepare his ship for deployment and the beleaguered civilian plant manager who tries to steer his charge through perilous, uncharted economic waters? In many ways, no, as both sound the clarion call for increased productivity, be it in the form of improved engineering reliability, or a more reliable widget off the assembly line.

The civilian manager and the peacetime military manager ashore exhibit the greatest similarities as they perform almost indistinguishable functions. It must be noted, however, that most unrestricted line naval officers serving in shore billets are either working in their subspecialties or merely between their primary assignments as seagoing naval officers.

It is as a manager in the fleet, attached to a ship, squadron, or submarine, that more pronounced differences begin to appear between the naval manager and his civilian counterpart. We note such possible differences as longer working hours, stricter accountability, and more responsibility but reject them as compelling differences because we feel the civilian manager faces many of the same conditions, albeit in different forms. We believe the single most compelling difference between civilian and seagoing managers is the more total relationship that exists between "the management and the employees" at sea. Especially on a deployment, management, in concert with leadership, is a 24-hour-a-day job for prolonged periods of time. For the manager at sea, a primary objective is optimum performance from each individual on board. Therefore, he must be concerned about everything that affects the sailor's performance, such as his food, habitability, training, liberty, personal appearance, financial status, and family. How many civilian managers have stood next to their men in a court of law? Many division officers have. A paternal watchful care for the comfort and welfare of his men is required to a far greater extent from the naval manager than from his civilian counterpart.

As an aside, the authors believe another significant, though smaller difference between the civilian and the naval manager is that the naval officer "going down to the sea in ships" simply has more plain, unadulterated fun. While we admit that some civilian jobs may be as enjoyable as going to sea, we seriously doubt it. Nevertheless, this belief shouldn't detract from the cogency of our thesis.

In summary, within the peacetime environment, although differences do exist especially for those managers at sea, the differences are a matter of degree and certainly not overwhelming. In peacetime, therefore, we conclude that the management paradigm prevails, and leadership can be considered an element of the overall management process.

But what about wartime? Just as in discussing a fireman's profession in which he may spend most of his time performing fire prevention duties but exists primarily to extinguish fires, any similar discussion of a naval officer, who may indeed spend most of his career performing war prevention duties, would be woefully incomplete unless the wartime dimensions of his profession were fully addressed.

When the focus of our attention shifts to wartime, the differences between the civilian and naval manager become more acute. As long as force and violence are the arbiters of national destiny, be it ours or that of any other nation, a need for the military shall exist. It cannot nor must not be forgotten that despite the degree of detente or the dialogue between past and present enemies, war remains the *raison d'etre* of the military. Although easily forgotten, the stark reality of future war underscores everything the naval officer does. No reasonable naval officer hopes for war because he will be among the first to enter the arena of battle. Nevertheless, we must prepare for the worst because it can occur with little warning.

Why is wartime managing different? The goal for the civilian manager remains largely the same—maximum productivity. For the naval manager, the measure of performance is that plus something more. It is life itself, his own and, more importantly, the lives of the men entrusted to him. And ultimately the stakes are the survival of our country, way of life, and families.

In wartime, management is not forgotten, but it is leadership which rises to dominate the wartime environment. The management process can prepare the military for war, and the importance of this should not be underestimated. But because of the sheer pressure and unpredictability of war, leadership must prevail. To condition subordinates to unhesitatingly risk their lives if need be, effective personal leadership is required, no—demanded! Management simply will not do this. In short then, leadership becomes the whole with management but an important subelement. It must be kept in mind that as leadership dominates the management process at sea in time of war, it also, although to a lesser extent, will gain in importance for the naval manager ashore.

In conclusion, it is not difficult for the young naval officer to comprehend the management and leadership paradigms and why each defines the management-leadership relationship as it does. As already mentioned, we think that in peacetime the relationship between management and leadership is nearly the same for civilian and naval managers. There would be no great harm in accepting the civilian viewpoint that leadership is a subelement of the management process—*as long as we did not have to go to war again*. But war (or the expectation of war) is the reason for the Navy's existence. War, or rather war prevention, is our business. And for that reason, leadership for the naval officer must be first in peacetime as well as in wartime. Just as an appendage long neglected will readily atrophy, the Navy cannot neglect the preeminence of leadership just because it happens to be operating in a peacetime environment. No switch exists that when pushed will automatically change the way the individual officer views himself, as a manager first or as a leader first. The Navy is culpable if the manager-leader identity crisis develops. It must be made clear to the young naval officer that he must, *at all times*, be a leader first.

This is not an easy task, for officers may spend 95% of their careers being peacetime civilian-type managers. Yet they must be prepared to be wartime leaders. How can the Navy prepare them? Leadership is not impersonal, analytical, or quantifiable and is therefore difficult to teach. Probably the best that can be hoped for is to emphasize its importance and to keep it uppermost in the minds of young naval officers. At the various schools where leadership is a part of the curriculum, visiting speakers should be invited to discuss leadership qualities and situations with the students. The young naval officer should be emphatically urged to take advantage of visiting speaker programs such as those sponsored by the Naval Institute or the Naval War College where great leaders of the past, both military and civilian, are often invited to speak. Commanding officers and executive officers should encourage discussions about leadership with their junior officers. Whatever the method of underscoring the importance of leadership, the essential thing is that the junior officer crystallize in his mind the relationship between management and leadership. This should be done at the expense of learning exotic new civilian management techniques.

Of course, as the saying goes, you can lead a horse to water, but you can't make him drink, meaning that we doubt a mandatory, lockstep leadership program would be effective. The most the Navy can realistically do is foster the proper atmosphere in which the study of leadership is cultivated and encouraged. Each junior officer must take it upon his own initiative to read and study leadership-related works. To quote Admiral Arleigh Burke, in the January 1975 *Proceedings*, "The easiest way to find what those [leadership] traits are and learn how to acquire them is by studying the leaders who have gone before." Certainly studying the lives of past great leaders, both military and civilian, would be of great benefit to every young naval officer.

In closing, we emphasize that we are not belittling management or those who specialize in the management field. We are not de-emphasizing the importance of the management process or of modern management techniques. On the contrary, we believe the Navy should avail itself of even more civilian management techniques, so long as they help us to better accomplish our mission. Nor are we saying that the function of the naval manager is inherently more important than that of the civilian manager, that we are somehow "better" than our civilian counterparts. But the naval manager *is* unique. He works in a very special environment toward very special ends. It is through a knowledge and understanding of his special *raison d'etre* that the junior naval officer can recognize that the management and leadership relationships in the two paradigms, though different, are not incompatible.

The young naval officer should always keep in mind, to paraphrase the opening lines of "Qualifications of a Naval Officer," often attributed to John Paul Jones, "It is by no means enough that a naval officer be a qualified manager, he must be that of course, but also a great deal more—he must be a *leader*."

5 "YOUNG OFFICERS AND LEADERSHIP"

ADM Arleigh Burke, USN (Ret.)

In 1976 the Vincent Astor Foundation and the Naval Institute created a unique opportunity and incentive for young officers to consider and write about naval leadership by creating an essay contest known as the Vincent Astor Memorial Leadership Essay Contest (VAMLEC). In addition to a substantial cash prize and a medallion, young officers were further encouraged to submit their VAMLEC essays by the inclusion of a short piece in *Proceedings* magazine by Admiral Arleigh Burke, a former Chief of Naval Operations (1955–1961) and well-known World War II figure who was admiringly known as "31-knot Burke" as a result of his high-speed destroyer tactics while commanding the legendary "Little Beaver Squadron."

"YOUNG OFFICERS AND LEADERSHIP"

By ADM Arleigh Burke, USN (Ret.), U.S. Naval Institute *Proceedings* (January 1975): 4.

Of all the many factors that go into producing success in a naval battle, the most important is the leadership of the commander.

Regardless of the old shibboleth, leaders are not born—they are developed. Some people have more aptitude than others; but no man becomes a great leader unless he develops within himself the traits necessary to a leader. The easiest way to find what those traits are and learn how to acquire them is by studying the leaders who have gone before.

Great leaders have much in common. Each of them had a goal, an objective they wanted to achieve. Usually naval leaders aspired to win honor and success for their country. Each of them worked hard to achieve a high degree of professionalism. Each tried to become the best naval officer among his peers. Each learned thoroughly all the elements of his profession. They knew the capability and limitations of the equipment they used—not superficially but thoroughly. They learned how to communicate with their fellow men, and to inspire their associates with the zeal and enthusiasm they themselves possessed. They realized that not only must they be highly skilled professionals, but so must all under their command.

They demanded high performance of their subordinates and trained their crews so that they were eager, enthusiastic, and, above all, skilled in the performance of their tasks. They recognized that no matter how great a leader a man might be, no man could lead a rabble or poorly trained subordinates to success. Well trained units can win naval actions without a great leader, but a great leader cannot be successful without trained, willing followers. Most of them studied their predecessors to emulate the characteristics of those who were successful and to avoid the traits of the unsuccessful.

Great leaders were not perfect. Each had his faults. These too should be recognized and shunned.

6 "THE CHALLENGE OF MORAL LEADERSHIP"

Capt Michael J. O'Hara, USMC

This article was awarded First Honorable Mention in the Vincent Astor Memorial Leadership Contest in 1977 for good reason. Besides being well-written with many quotable passages, it draws on relevant portions of foundational sources such as *Navy Regulations*, the *Uniform Code of Military Justice*, the *Marine Corps Manual*, and *The Naval Officer's Guide*. It is laced with wisdom drawn from Greek philosopher Socrates, famed Army combat historian S. L. A. Marshall, legendary Marine commandant John A. Lejeune, and classical author of *The Canterbury Tales*, Geoffrey Chaucer. O'Hara equates morality with responsibility in terms of leadership and takes a fundamental approach toward attaining and maintaining the components that make up that indispensable trait.

"THE CHALLENGE OF MORAL LEADERSHIP"

By Capt Michael J. O'Hara, USMC, U.S. Naval Institute *Proceedings* (August 1977): 58–62.

A few years ago a group of experts met in Washington to discuss the question, "Can America survive the next war?" They were concerned primarily with whether a large, industrialized, technologically dependent nation could recover from the damage which would ensue from a major nuclear attack. Although their conclusions were guardedly optimistic, they limited discussion to physical survival and virtually ignored the less visible, but no less important, damage that would be done to the spiritual fabric of society. This is not surprising since ours is a society which is much more comfortable with analysis and measurement than it is with such abstract and frustratingly imprecise concepts as duty, responsibility, and morality.

As the naval service becomes increasingly more dependent on technology, its officers may well be increasingly tempted to give in to that same tendency to judge success in terms of systems efficiency—the managerial dimension—rather than in terms of personal values. The inclination to do so already exists. Inspections at all levels of command regularly zero in on the measurable. "People programs" notwithstanding, such criteria as reporting error rates, equipment readiness statistics, and stock inventory levels often become the index by which an officer's fitness for command is evaluated. No doubt these criteria are vitally important within the context of any complex organization, but the danger arises when the system is emphasized at the expense of the men and women who make it work.

Without getting into the "leader" *vs.* "manager" debate, I believe it is fair to state that although the leader and manager both must concern themselves with systems efficiency and organizational effectiveness, the manager regards people primarily as a factor in the equation of goal attainment while the leader must regard them as ends in themselves. In fact, this latter approach lies at the very foundation of traditional military leadership.

The responsibilities of leadership are perhaps greater today than they ever have been in the past. In addition to mastering vast quantities of information, the modern leader must be prepared to deal with a better educated, more articulate subordinate who is often skeptical of authority. The responsibilities, however, remain the same though some are less difficult than others because their effects are measurable. To ensure that subordinates are adequately fed, clothed, and berthed is relatively simple because the results are apparent. Knowledge can be tested, and performance evaluated. However, the leader's responsibility for the moral welfare of his men is altogether more difficult because its results are intangible and hinge directly on what he is, not on what he knows or says. To project the proper image is the most fundamental and challenging of a leader's responsibilities.

U.S. Navy Regulations, under "Requirement for Exemplary Conduct," states:

> All commanding officers and others in authority in the naval service are required to show in themselves a good example of virtue, honor, patriotism and subordination; to be vigilant in inspecting the conduct of all persons who are placed under their command; to guard against and suppress all dissolute and immoral practices, and to correct, according to the laws and regulations of the Navy, all persons who are guilty of them; and to take all necessary and proper measures, under the laws, regulations and customs of the naval service, to promote and safeguard the morale, the physical well-being, and the general welfare of the officers and enlisted persons under their command or charge. (10 USC 5947)

It is significant that this requirement is placed not on the Inspector General, the chaplain, or the senior enlisted man, but on the commanding officer or others in authority. Yet sometimes, it seems, the requirement is not met, and there is a reason why.

The moral revolution, which has taken place throughout the world during the past 15 years, has challenged some of the basic tenets of Judeo-Christian ethics. Values once held so sacred as to be unquestionable have been freely and publicly scorned to the point where even those with a strongly developed moral sense have felt the stirrings of self-doubt. The process has not been entirely bad, however. Values which are adhered to through the influence of tradition are bound to be weaker and less effective than those which are held as the result of experience and reflection. So the attacks on traditional ethics have served a useful purpose in that they have forced people to reexamine their moral premises and reevaluate their beliefs. But this is an essentially negative reaction to a problem which deserves a more positive approach. It is too easy to slip into a "fortress mentality" and insist that what is traditional is right because it is traditional. Socrates laid down the first principle of philosophy when he said, "The unexamined life is not worth living," and perhaps it is the most traditional, the most dearly held beliefs that need to be examined first, then reaffirmed, modified, or even rejected if it is discovered that they have lost their currency. This seems to be what is happening in the world today. Certainly not all who question traditional values are moral anarchists. When men of good will can be found on both sides of such questions as homosexuality and abortion, to name only two of the more controversial, then something profoundly important is happening.

Whether the outcome of the struggle will be the triumph of traditionalism or some blending of traditional and modern ideas, it is impossible to say. But one effect of the struggle is already clear. As the tempo of the attack on established values has intensified, people in general, military officers among them, have become less sure of their moral premises and consequently more prone to tolerate violations of time-honored standards of moral behavior. Yet the requirement of exemplary conduct remains, clear and unequivocal. An officer in the naval service is required not only to set the example, but to create a healthy moral climate in which the men and women under his charge can develop their characters to the fullest. The role of the leader assumes even greater importance when we consider that the struggle between Communism and democracy is not merely a rivalry between two political and economic systems, but a conflict between two diametrically opposed views of the nature and worth of the human spirit. If we prevail, it will be due less to the potency of our armaments than to the strength of our spirit. This is the greatest challenge of moral leadership.

Law and regulation lay down our responsibilities in this area, but to carry them out intelligently and effectively, we must understand them. Basically there are two sources for our concept of morality: religion and philosophy (or ethics).[1] The religious concept of morality is based on the premises that man has been created by God and placed on earth to aid in the fulfillment of a divine plan; that the trials of life are a test which, if passed, will merit eternal reward; and that during the course of his life man is expected to observe certain moral precepts which will make him pleasing in the sight of God. Although God works through human nature and not against it, so that to be truly good is to be truly human, religious morality is still essentially authoritarian. Obedience to the divine will is the main requirement. Morality based on philosophy or ethics, on the other hand, takes man as its starting point and asks what is the nature of man and how must he act to be true to it. These questions have been asked and answered by philosophers from the time of man's first reflection on his condition. Although there has been a wide divergence of opinion over the ages, certain basic principles have been agreed upon: (1) man has a nature—that is, there is something unique to man which distinguishes him from all other living and nonliving things; (2) man can know his nature—that is, he can recognize that he is something separate and apart from the rest of creation and that what differentiates him is his capacity for thought; (3) man can know that he should live and act in accordance with his nature—that is, he has a moral sense; and (4) man can live and act in accordance with his nature—that is, he has the ability to make right moral choices.

These four principles are the basis of that natural law which holds that "good" is that which advances man's nature; "evil" is that which retards it. Different philosophers at different times have challenged the theory, but it has been unusually persistent, mostly because it makes sense. To deny it requires the assumption either that man's nature is intrinsically evil and that "good" is therefore unnatural or anti-human, or that man has no nature, or if he has, he cannot know it. Both assumptions reduce the human condition to an absurdity. We treat plants differently than we do animals because we have learned from experience what it takes to raise each to its highest level of development. In other words, each has a nature and we know what it is. To say that we can know the lesser orders of existence, and yet not know ourselves, however imperfectly, is illogical and contradicted by experience.

Once we accept the theory, we are faced with the question of what constitutes the good which advances man's nature. There are many possible answers, but the best and simplest is that those things are good which allow a man to develop his potential as a man. Most answers to philosophical questions lead immediately to still more questions, and it is beyond the scope of this essay to deal with the question of what it means to be a man. It is enough to say that our form of government is based on the premise that man is a creature endowed with the inalienable rights of life, liberty, and the pursuit of happiness and that the purpose of government is to ensure that he has the opportunity to exercise those rights within a social context. Rights imply responsibilities, and since the context in which we operate is social, we exercise our rights and carry out our responsibilities with respect to others as well as ourselves. Responsibilities, of course, vary in degree. The responsibility of parent for child or teacher for student is greater than that of neighbor for neighbor. It hinges in large part on the extent to which one is dependent on the other. The dependence of the led on the leader is greater in the military service than in any other profession. Consequently the responsibility of the military leader is greater. Having sworn to defend the Constitution, he is required to do so not only in a purely military sense, but also by exemplifying and upholding the moral principles on which the Constitution is based. He is, in short, required to be a gentleman.

The word "gentleman" is not easy to define with any precision and perhaps no definition could do the concept full justice. The *Manual for Courts-Martial* defines it by its antithesis when it states, "There are certain moral attributes common to the ideal officer and the perfect gentleman, a lack of which is indicated by acts of dishonesty or unfair dealing, of indecency or indecorum, or of lawlessness, injustice, or cruelty." Fortunately we are not expected to be paragons of virtue, for as the article continues, "Not everyone is or can be expected to meet ideal moral standards, but there is a limit of tolerance below which the individual standards of an officer . . . cannot fall without seriously compromising his standing as an officer . . . or his character as a gentleman." This is not an abstract ideal to be pursued for its own sake, nor is it merely a reflection of the aristocratic origin of so many military traditions. It is a fundamental guide to practical, effective leadership.

To be effective, an officer must have character, which is simply the strength of will to do what is required when some other course of action might be more attractive. Character can be developed only through practice, through a long series of individual acts of the will, the end result of which is dependability. There is probably no more essential leadership trait. "An officer without character," as General S. L. A. Marshall wrote, "is more useless than a ship with no bottom."[2] To be effective an officer must inspire the respect of his subordinates, not only by his professional competence, but by his personal integrity as well. If he shows a weakness for alcohol or gambling or women, he will be perceived as weak in other areas and the respect he needs to lead will diminish accordingly. Finally, to be truly effective, an officer must set the example in such a way that he becomes a role-model for his subordinates. He will be one in any case, for good or ill. The standard he sets will be the one they emulate. But only if he demands the best of his men in behavior and conduct, by showing the way himself, will they be psychologically and morally prepared for the stress and danger they might someday face in war. The practical effect of good example is good discipline, a point well made in the following excerpt from the *Naval Officer's Guide*:[3]

> *Good example* on the part of officers is one of the prime requisites to maintenance of good discipline. In fact, it is no exaggeration to say that the true, desirable brand of discipline can neither be instilled nor maintained unless the officers *practice what they preach*. Our men are too intelligent and too high-spirited to extend respect and loyalty to men of hypocrisy, insincerity, and sham.

Character, integrity, and good example are traits of a gentleman. A leader who does not possess them is, in fact, no leader at all whatever billet or rank he may hold. They are also moral qualities, practical in that the extent to which they are present in a command, among officers and men alike, stands in direct relation to the level of morale and respect for authority. In their absence, a unit will suffer not only a loss in morale, discipline, and efficiency, but also will be seriously compromised in its ability to carry out its mission. There can be no more practical reason for insisting that officers be gentlemen.

Moral leadership is difficult because, as stated earlier, it depends on what a man is. No amount of reading, study, or reflection will make an officer morally fit unless it is accompanied by a conscious, unremitting effort at self-improvement. Moral living is not passive. It is more than just not doing bad things. It is an active process of personal struggle against weakness, expediency, and self-doubt, and its rewards are strength of character, resolution, and confidence. The officer who is unwilling to make the effort himself has no right to demand it of his men.

Moral leadership is especially difficult today because modern society has slipped its ethical moorings. We live in an age of skepticism toward all traditional values, and even the churches no longer enjoy the respect they once had. It is not surprising, then, that many of the young people coming into the service today are resistant to authority and resent any attempt to modify their behavior in the direction of what they see as establishment norms. Much of the fault is ours. We have recruited them with promises of education, adventure, travel, and "fun," and it isn't until after they have committed themselves that they learn that duty is a hard, exacting taskmaster. Some of them feel cheated, or at least deceived, and so become more resistant. Perhaps that is the inevitable result of trying to sell service to country as if it were toothpaste. On the bright side, most young servicemen are as idealistic as they have ever been, although they often go to great lengths to hide it. Their skepticism is a kind of defense mechanism against what they regard as the hypocrisy of society. Fortunately, few of them are cynical. Cynicism seems to be a disease of age and experience. They can still be reached by officers who are willing to show them the way. Those who come from stable homes where they received strong moral guidance from their parents will expect the same from their officers. But those whose backgrounds have been unstable are in the greatest need of positive guidance. Though they won't admit it and may not even be consciously aware of it, they want it. Since human nature tends toward the good, an appeal to a man's best instincts usually will not fail.

Next to personal example, the most essential ingredient of successful moral leadership is a proper relationship between an officer and his subordinates. What that relationship should be was perhaps best expressed by Major General

John A. Lejeune, 13th Commandant of the Marine Corps, when, in paragraph 5390.0 of the *Marine Corps Manual*, he wrote:

> The relation between officers and enlisted men should in no sense be that of superior and inferior nor that of master and servant, but rather that of teacher and scholar. In fact, it should partake of the nature of the relation between father and son, to the extent that officers, especially commanders, are responsible for the physical, mental, and moral welfare, as well as the discipline and military training of the men under their command who are serving the Nation in the Marine Corps.

Although he should be the embodiment of personal virtue, an officer will be totally ineffective in his role as a moral leader if he projects an attitude of superiority. His men will be quick to sense and resent it. This is not to say that he must compromise his personal or professional standards or pretend to be less than he is. On the contrary, as a leader he is expected to be better than the men he leads. But as a moral man he will be acutely aware that character is formed not over days and weeks, but over years, and he will approach his task with the humility that comes from an appreciation of his own human weakness. And he will never forget that his goal is not to make saints of soldiers, but to develop disciplined fighting men who will stand up under the rigors of combat.

According to one of the popular clichés of the '60s, the military is a microcosm of society. The phrase was repeated so often that many came to believe it even though it is true only in a limited sense. Certainly young men and women do not shed their problems along with their civilian clothes when they arrive at boot camp or OCS, and if drug abuse and racial discrimination are problems in the civilian community, they will be problems in the military as well. But a military organization is in no sense simply a mirror-image of the society from which it draws its members. It is an institution with a unique set of values and a code of ethics all its own. Therein lies its strength. While attitudes toward moral issues within society at large periodically swing from conservative to liberal and back again, depending on the prevailing climate of opinion, the military remains constant in its adherence to traditional values. As an institution, the military is inherently conservative, in the root sense of the word; that is, its function is to conserve, as well as to defend, the principles on which the nation was founded. In many ways this makes it easier for the officer to carry out his moral leadership responsibilities. Working within a closed society, he is less subject to the winds of change blowing in the outside world. Along with his commission he has accepted a moral and ethical code which it becomes his duty to live by and inculcate in his subordinates. If he has a strong religious faith, then the support he will derive from it will be inestimable, but even if he lacks that kind of faith, the code will be his source of strength.

Much more could be said on the subject of moral leadership, particularly in the area of its practical application. Drug and alcohol abuse, racial discrimination, and financial irresponsibility are a few of the problems which demand the leader's attention in the day-to-day performance of his duties. The more general problems of conduct in time of war might also have been addressed. But I considered it more useful to reemphasize fundamentals. The leader who adopts them as the basis of his personal ethic usually will not have trouble applying them in any situation.

Morality is simply another word for responsibility—responsibility to oneself and to others, but it is not uniquely the concern of the leader. It is the concern of every man and woman who wants to be truly human. For the military leader, however, it assumes particular importance since his sole reason for being is to set the example for others, to show them the way, to *lead*. In the words of the poet Chaucer, "If gold ruste, what shal iren do?" For all its difficulties, the burden of moral leadership will be gladly borne by any officer who recognizes its significance. This is the challenge and the reward.

Notes

1. See Leo R. Ward, *Ethics: A College Text* (New York: Harper & Row, 1965), 142–143.
2. See S. L. A. Marshall, *The Officer as a Leader* (Harrisburg: Stackpole, 1966).
3. See Arthur A. Ageton and William P. Mack, *The Naval Officer's Guide*, 8th Edition (Annapolis, Maryland: United States Naval Institute, 1970).

7 "CLOSING THE GAPS IN NAVAL LEADERSHIP"

LT James Stavridis, USN

Long before Jim Stavridis rose to the pinnacle of naval leadership as a four-star admiral, he was wielding the pen as well as the sword. He is a legend at the Naval Institute for a wide variety of reasons, not least of which is that he published articles and books at every rank during his storied career. This article, which earned him a First Honorable Mention in the Vincent Astor Memorial Leadership Essay Contest in 1982, defines two fundamental approaches to leadership—charismatic and administrative—and effectively argues that both have validity and relevance to naval leaders. He also warns that serious problems can arise when the two styles "act in opposition in a chain of command," creating a deleterious gap.

"CLOSING THE GAPS IN NAVAL LEADERSHIP"

By LT James Stavridis, USN, U.S. Naval Institute *Proceedings* (July 1982): 76–78.

Leadership is both an art and a science with many intricate facets. Yet there are two fundamental approaches to leadership; I have termed these *charismatic* and *administrative*. Charismatic leaders influence the attitudes, perceptions, and beliefs of the follower. Administrative leaders, on the other hand, directly control the actions of the follower. When these widely divergent leadership techniques both appear in a chain of command, gaps can occur, causing many of the leadership problems in the fleet.

To function in the naval milieu, a leader must have some administrative ability, even if the predominant tendency is toward a charismatic approach, and vice versa. The two basic styles of leadership are typical of the current state of fleet leadership. Of course, the categories of leaders are not black-and-white. History provides examples of a widely disparate group of leaders; as Lieutenant Thomas B. Grassey observed in his leadership essay "Outcomes, Essences, and Individuals" (*Proceedings*, July 1976, p. 73), "what one sees when one . . . scan[s] history for the unique elements common to great leaders is *nothing*." This is because of the subtleties of style; yet leadership can almost always be grouped in one of the two categories.

Leadership is defined in General Order 21 as the "art of accomplishing the Navy's mission through people. It is the sum of those qualifications of intellect, human understanding, and moral character that enable a man to inspire and to manage a group of people successfully." "To inspire and to manage": these are the operative words in the definition; they define the categories of leaders in the naval service. Echoing this thought, Lieutenant R. T. E. Bowler III and Lieutenant D. R. Bowler, in discussing the distinction between a leader and a manager, stated that "within the Navy today, two philosophical paradigms are competing" ("The Naval Officer: Manager or Leader," *Proceedings*, December 1975, p. 64). The Navy today has its share of both charismatic leaders, who are capable of inspiring those under them, and administrative leaders, who effectively manage their men.

Either of the two styles of leadership, or better yet, a combination of the two, can be effective. However, when the two styles act in opposition in a chain of command, great problems can arise, signals may be missed from above and below in the chain of command, and failed mission readiness may occur. This sort of failure is often put down to a lack of leadership; in reality, it is often a result of gaps in the leadership chain. Neither style of leadership is necessarily more effective. The Navy needs leaders with both sorts of abilities to fulfill all its missions in peace and war.

A charismatic leader can change the way others think, and thus influence the way they act. He can make sure not only that his men arrive on time, but that they *want* to arrive on time. The charismatic leader uses tools that change the perceptions of his followers. Such abilities are, to a degree, innate, but can also be developed through training in the understanding of human character and by practice. The charismatic leader is capable of influencing attitudes as well as actions. He will probably exhibit some of the following traits: uses personal examples often, attempts to understand the motivation and background of his men, acts on intuition or initiative in problem solving, and exhibits great trust in his men.

On the other hand, an administrative leader is more concerned with the external actions of his men than with changing their inner motivations. He tends to believe that the key ingredients of the leadership problem revolve around hard knowledge, training, rigid scheduling, and frequent inspections. In the January 1981 *Proceedings*, page 82, Admiral Hyman G. Rickover, U.S. Navy (Ret.), summarized everything necessary to know about leadership in a few lines:

a. Learn your job
b. Work hard at your job
c. Train your people
d. Inspect frequently to see that the job is being done properly.

For our purposes, a definition of the administrative leader would be: An actor capable of attention to details of time, place, and mission demand, who directs his men in achieving the mission by ensuring control over their external actions. He probably exhibits the following traits: places distance between himself and subordinates on a personal level, is concerned primarily with the details of each operation, prefers great detail in the preparation for and the solving of problems, does not easily deviate from proposed operations, approaches problems from a management perspective, and conducts frequent inspections.

One problem that naval leaders must face is the gap that occurs when the two styles of leadership act in opposition in the chain of command. Both types of leaders can exist in the same chain of command, particularly in a relatively small organization, such as a ship, submarine, or squadron. When these styles work in opposition to each other the resulting conflict can be at the center of a number of leadership problems.

As Powell Fraser correctly observed in his essay "Leading the Leaders" *(Proceedings,* July 1977, p. 79), "Today's leadership problem may be that the senior's enthusiasm is not readily apparent to the junior officers." Such an argument can be extended to cover not only the relations between junior officers and their seniors, but also to cover the gap between administrators and charismatics. When a junior in the chain of command is confronted with a leadership approach with which he is unfamiliar, he can become confused. If he feels constrained to imitate it, and is not comfortable or effective, he can become disillusioned. This situation can arise with either charismatics or administrators at the top of the pyramid as shown here:

Petty Officer Jones is an E-5 boiler technician on an Atlantic fleet carrier. He is a charismatic leader; he directs the men assigned to him by influencing their attitudes and beliefs with personal contact and example. He leads from the deck plates. Morale is high despite the arduous conditions of aircraft carrier engineering.

Master Chief Franklin is the leading chief petty officer (CPO) for the 190-man electrical (E) division of a West Coast carrier. He is primarily an administrative leader; he has daily meetings with his ten work center supervisors; he has concise managerial control of all personnel through his meticulous record system; and he gives personal attention to all details of the E division operation. He conducts frequent inspections of personnel, spaces, berthing, and equipment, but maintains a personal distance.

Lieutenant Smith is the combat systems officer of a Pacific Fleet destroyer. He controls his 80-man division through charismatic leadership techniques, including open give-and-take with his four division officers, personal contact with the men in his department, occasional department head call with his troops, and recognition for a job well done. He leads "from the inside out," and attempts to motivate his men by understanding their perceptions and beliefs.

Commander Drake is the commanding officer (CO) of an East Coast destroyer. He is an administrative leader who requires detailed plan of actions and milestones (POA&M) reports for all events, works almost exclusively through his executive officer, sends weekly memos to his department heads, and wants the ship run by the book. He is a first-class manager and organizer, concerned with preparation, planning, and direct regulation of the actions of his subordinates. His ship is an "E" winner with high morale.

Suppose Commander Drake is the CO of a destroyer, with Lieutenant Smith as his combat systems officer, Master Chief Franklin as the leading CPO for the department, and Petty Officer Jones as the leading petty officer (LPO) for the operations specialist (OS) gang. The CO, being an administrative leader, has a policy on the ship of insisting on a detailed, daily POA&M being submitted in preparation for all inspections. Lieutenant Smith understands the CO's requirement for a POA&M for the pending planned maintenance system (PMS) inspection, but also feels that personal contact in the form of spot-checks and a general motivational approach will get his men ready for the inspection. Franklin is tasked with preparing the POA&M, which he does with great enthusiasm and administrative acumen. He is not impressed with what he regards as Smith's overly familiar approach with the men; Jones, on the other hand, regards Franklin's carefully prepared POA&M as a waste of time and a typical example of the paperwork that absorbs his time as LPO. The crosscurrents in the chain of command indicate friction between virtually all parties. In private conversation with the CO, Franklin subtly makes his feeling known on Smith's "new style" leadership. Smith overhears Jones grumbling about Franklin and his "paperwork Navy." The whole chain of command is at odds, even though they all share the same basic goal: combat readiness. Sound familiar? After the ship fails the PMS inspection, Jones is upbraided for his lack of attention to the POA&M; Franklin is hammered for "not getting the people psyched up for the inspection"; and Smith is called on the carpet for his lack of enthusiasm in implementing the POA&M. The CO is left wondering about the efficiency of his entire organization. Such are the gaps in naval leadership through which fall inspections, recruiting efforts, morale, and entire commands. The ultimate loser is the Navy.

There are several solutions to this type of leadership conflict. The first, and in some ways the most feasible, is the simplest: The CO of a unit sets the tone and pace of the organization, and it is up to the command leaders to adapt and make sure they are not working at cross-purposes with the CO's approach. This is the solution some segments of the Navy have used for a long time. This stops up the gaps by forcing all the leaders in the command into roughly the same approach. The advantages of this technique are its simplicity, traditional acceptance of the CO's complete command, and its ease of implementation. Several disadvantages exist in this method as well, however. First of all, it can over-direct leadership training in a single style, producing frustrated or ineffective junior leaders struggling with a leadership style alien to them. This leads to low leader morale, retention problems, and production of relatively ineffective leaders. Second, history and analysis show that the Navy needs leaders who are both charismatic and administrative to handle the wide variety of missions. Our leaders must develop both styles, and the only way to learn is to act. As Lieutenant Grassey observed in his leadership essay in the July 1976 *Proceedings*, page 75, about how one becomes a leader, "For proficiency, doing it is far better than reading about it."

Another approach to the problem is possible. The ideal leader would be one who combines the attributes of a charismatic and an administrator. The ideal solution to the hypothetical situation would be for the CO to foster an environment in which his junior leaders (including officers, CPOs, and POs) become solid administrators and develop charismatic qualities as well. In the example, Smith should pursue his techniques, but fulfill the CO's requirements for POA&Ms as well; in the process, he would develop in both directions. At the same time, Smith should be encouraging Franklin to spend time on the deck plates working directly with his men. While in the process, the E-9 could probably sit down with Jones and begin to teach him the fundamental skills of administration that are so crucial to his advancement through the rates. The best solution would be a command in which the overall tone encouraged development on both sides of the leadership spectrum, with all the players contributing their individual skills and acumen. This environment presupposes some attention to the styles of leadership, open and realistic evaluations of performance and results, and a willingness on the part of all hands to learn from the chain of command.

Given as a premise that the Navy has an interest in developing leaders who can perform both administrative and charismatic functions, and that the best method of becoming a better leader is to get in there and lead people, a case can be made for the following proposals:

- recognize that everyone has the same basic goal: combat readiness
- continue to use the leadership and management training (LMET) school system to explore the elements of the two basic leadership styles
- investigate the possibility of a CPO course for POs making the transition from E-6 to E-7; for many, this is a transition from an essentially charismatic to an administrative situation
- continue to teach basic leadership theory in the officer procurement courses, emphasizing toleration for other styles and the need to find what works best, as well as the development of a wide range of leadership skills
- cross train leaders by conscious assignment to positions that demand a different style of leadership than the leader has used in the past, i.e., rotation from Communications Officer to First Lieutenant, from collateral duty jobs with different emphasis, within division for the POs and CPOs
- encourage the use of leadership techniques that can train in both charismatic and administrative ways: an inspection can become a means of learning more about the juniors in the chain
- insofar as combat readiness and safety allow, be willing to allow inexperienced leaders time to discover what works best for them

- use informal means of training leaders, i.e., the best single source of information and guidance for the division officer is often the division leading chief through informal counseling at the E-7/0-1 level
- communicate and tolerate; there are many ways to do the same job.

For some time, the debate has been one of leader versus manager, or of charisma versus administration. We can and should be instead striving for a leader who is *both* charismatic and a fine administrator. If we open our eyes and train both aspects of our leaders, it is the Navy that will benefit. There is a place for charisma and a place for administration; but both sides must work and develop together to ensure that we can close the gap in naval leadership.

8 "LEADERSHIP: SOME SOUNDINGS"

LT Thomas F. Marfiak, USN

Another First Honorable Mention in the Vincent Astor Memorial Leadership Contest, Lieutenant Marfiak's discussion of necessary leadership traits is appropriately "salted" with nautical terminology. But there is more than a Sailor's touch to this piece. He is joined in his discussion by the likes of Francis Bacon, Xenophon, and Horatio Nelson, yet this is no mere "ivory tower" approach to the subject. While relying on classical literature and history to make his points, he nonetheless proffers pragmatic advice. Among his offerings are sound leadership principles, such as "reciprocal respect" and suitable aphorisms such as "let us who would lead temper unremitting discipline with a measure of compassion."

"LEADERSHIP: SOME SOUNDINGS"

By LT Thomas F. Marfiak, USN, U.S. Naval Institute *Proceedings* (August 1975): 80–82.

In the presence of leadership, we are aware that it exists, yet, like some rare element not yet completely analyzed by science, we are at a loss to define its separate elements. Even supposing that we were to agree on the constituent parts, what long discussions are still possible on their proportions? Yet, who better than naval officers *should* know what makes up the matter of leadership? So, like the ancient philosophers, starting from crude notions of fire, water, earth, and the heavens, let us begin a voyage to discover the elements of leadership—a voyage which can only give us a deeper knowledge of ourselves.

Unlike so many unexplained phenomena that remain within the confines of scientific research, leadership has the signal advantage of being examined and experienced by every one of us—leadership is real. As with oxygen, we know almost immediately when it is lacking or nonexistent. It is equally apparent, moreover, that leadership presupposes the existence of people wanting, needing to be led. Indeed, the critical element of effective leadership is the quality of the relationship between the leader and his followers. In the context of a military organization this is transformed into the relationship between the commander and those men for whom he is responsible. The efficiency of this relationship is dependent on reciprocal one: on the one hand, the commander, who exercises leadership; on the other hand, those members of his organization, be it ship or shore, who recognize his leadership and, in so doing, permit the effective functioning of the whole.

The officer who is not familiar with the legendary exploits of Admiral Nelson, and who cannot at least recite trilogy of the Nile, Copenhagen, and Trafalgar victories, is hopefully rare. But to illustrate this reciprocal care that is a prerequisite of effective leadership, the events following Nelson's departure from Gibraltar on 11 February 1797, while less well known, speaks volumes. Having collected his two lieutenants, Culverhouse and Hardy, recently released from Spanish custody, Nelson weighed anchor in the forenoon and soon found himself pursued by two Spanish ships of the line and a frigate. The chase was on. However, relative speed being only slightly to the enemy's advantage, there appeared to be time to conduct dinner in a gentlemanly manner.

No sooner had they begun when the "man overboard" cry ended further conversation. Lieutenant Hardy, just freed, found himself officer-in-charge of the boat put off to search for the missing crew member. The current in the straits carried the rescue launch toward the pursuers so rapidly that, when no sign of the missing man was found, it seemed impossible for the launch and her crew to avoid capture. The crew pulled mightily to regain the *Minerve*, but no progress seemed evident. *Le Terrible* was almost within gunshot. "By God!" exclaimed Nelson, "I'll not lose Hardy! Back that mizzen-topsail." The action calls to mind Admiral Mitscher's famous "lights on" order to assist aircraft returning from the attack on Ozawa's carrier force nearly a century and a half later in the battle of the Philippine Sea. The sequel? Superior shiphandling and the onset of night combined to complete the rescue. When, years later, Vice Admiral Sir Thomas Masterton Hardy reflected on the man he had been privileged to serve, he no doubt accorded considerable credit to that day.

The lesson, taken from a now romanticized era, is no less applicable today. Within the bounds of technical specialization imposed by the increasing complexity of shipboard systems, the tendency is all too often to plead mounting paperwork and insufficient time as excuses for not making a decision. The effect remains invariably constant. The people we are expected to lead, the people who look to their officers for a minimum of personal concern, are left unsatisfied. Left to the conflicting currents of personal qualifications, family cares, and working conditions often beyond a sailor's power to correct, is it difficult to understand why he occasionally strays from the approved path? We must ask ourselves what we can do to restore our own effectiveness as well as his confidence in the essential merit of a system based on mutual respect. We must, in short, find a way to "back the mizzen-topsail," if that is what it takes.

Obviously the great Nelson felt that he could flaunt his seamanship and his crew in front of the enemy's nose, especially if it meant saving a valued member of his team; another component of leadership would therefore appear to be a certain professional knowledge. Timidity is often based on ignorance. It is no accident that retention rates have long been higher in the nuclear-power and aviation arms of the fleet while the surface officer retention rate hovers between the abysmally poor and the barely acceptable. Training—the ability to meet the challenge with a certain amount of knowledge—has been a prerequisite in these "other" areas.

We have, however, too long assumed that a young officer can walk on board his first ship armed with a knowledge of PMS and make it go. The progress made in the institution of the Surface Warfare Officer Schools is a considerable step forward in offering the surface officer the training he needs and desires. There is so much more, however, yet to be done.

Yet, were there no schools at all or money to develop new programs, the problem could still be attacked by improving the contact and communication (not synonymous terms) between division officers and petty officers. It is through these vital individuals that leadership must pass to be effective, to transform itself from objective and ideal to accomplishment and reality. Unfortunately, for a variety of reasons, the chain frequently breaks down here. Yet nowhere is the reciprocal respect inherent in true leadership more important.

Speaking in another context, former Secretary of Defense Thomas Gates once said that while civilians could not hope to match the accumulated professional expertise of the military community, they should, nonetheless, not be afraid to exercise their authority over the military when the nation's interests so dictate. In the same respect, but on a more microcosmic scale, the young division officer, whatever his specialization, should not unquestioningly assume that superior technical knowledge equals superior judgment. At the same time, should he be blessed with a calm and experienced professional chief petty officer, let him pay attention to the accumulated wisdom that even Secretary Gates would not have disputed. The exercise of judgment needs to be continuous and informed to be effective.

Yet the magical equation of leadership, this reciprocal respect between the leader and those men and women he leads, is only the beginning. The second element of leadership lies wholly within ourselves. We can broadly define this second and equally important component as the worthiness of the leader himself. "It is by no means enough that an officer be a gentleman," wrote John Paul Jones; the elements that compose the rest of his famous treatise, clothed in the modern idiom, may still speak clearly to us all.

First, we would seek personal honor fashioned of clear positions intelligently taken on every question, be it minor or complex. Let us take care that our bureaucratic affiliation does not offer a convenient excuse to model ourselves on the marvelous chameleon, changing our colors as the background dictates, until, for lack of a discernible goal, those whom we would lead lose interest.

Next, let's recognize that this incredibly rapid changing society we are part of is prone to produce a large degree of incertitude among us all, but especially among the young people who form the backbone of the fleet. With this knowledge, let us who would lead temper unremitting discipline with a measure of compassion.

In addition, whatever our rank, wherever we serve, if we would lead well, let's watch ourselves lest we be classed with Cassius as "lean and hungry" men. It is well to be disciplined, excellent to be professional, and superb to be dedicated to the task at hand. However none of these factors, or any others, should exclude one's sense of humor. We are all wary of the man who never laughs.

While a final point related to the leader's worthiness might be interpreted as a superfluous addition, it needs to be said: a leader is first someone we see. Let his dress, manners, and speech inspire emulation. Can we follow a man who by his very carriage urges defeat and resignation? An affirmative answer is doubtful and the lesson is obvious.

A third essential element of leadership is knowledge. Francis Bacon, writing during the reign of Elizabeth I, emphasized the desirability of a liberal knowledge as an asset to leaders. His account of Alexander the Great's profound respect for the glories of ancient Greek letters shows us that an open mind and eager spirit are not misplaced in military leaders. The expansion of knowledge, and especially the quantitative advances of technical knowledge, that surrounds us has made us all specialists, will it or not. Certainly, while we must all be competent within the area of our particular specialty or subspecialty, is it not reasonable to expect of a leader today, in an era when the role of the military within our democratic society is being questioned and examined with intensity, to be at least conversant with the principal issues of our time?

The leader, if we suppose the answer to be yes, owes it to himself as well as to his command, be it a squad, division, or fleet, to actively seek knowledge, to read, to question, to listen, and finally, if only during the long quiet hours of a midwatch, to reflect. This is no easy or quickly met task. It is a continuing effort, too often foregone, and the more easily foregone because it is so rarely encouraged by the professional environment in which we operate.

Experience shows, time and again, that whether we labor in the administrative maze of Washington or the clash and clamor of the flight deck, that problems present themselves so insistently that they effectively eliminate the most determined effort to set aside time to reflect upon the basic questions, to seek long-term solutions, and to investigate the long-range impacts. Yet those are precisely the actions expected of a leader, to foresee, to provide, and to be, in short, concerned, not only with today, but with tomorrow and the day after tomorrow as well. To be concerned, not only with the state of his equipment, but most especially with the state of his men. In any discussion of what leadership is, whatever the level of abstraction, we are invariably drawn back to the most essential element—man.

From Xenophon, marching with his troops across a hostile country, to Nelson, caring not only for the devoted Hardy but also for every man in his fleet, the most successful leaders have been, and continue to be, those who, despite the heavy fire, be it bullets or directives from higher authority, have known how to care for their men. I do not mean caring in a paternalistic sense, but rather in the sense of a mutual understanding, openly arrived at, in which a healthy concern for the rights of others is mingled with an unfailing sense of duty.

For, if we were by some fascinating interplay of science and morality to place a mirror before the image of leadership itself, we would see reflected there not leadership but duty. Far more than an outmoded concept, gathering dust and respect in a museum echoing with memories of long-silent carronades, duty is still very much with us. Duty is the keel upon which any assessment of leadership must be built. Without a sense of duty, however resourceful a leader be, he is nothing—a derelict. But let him be dedicated to an ideal, to the maintenance of a set of values that are to him as vital as life itself, and he is unconquerable.

Yet duty, like leadership, has several distinguishable components. Duty to ourselves, to adopt an egocentric reference, implies that we will do all in our power to develop whatever natural talents we possess, seeking new knowledge to complement acquired skills, as Bacon recommended. It also implies whatever personal moral and religious beliefs we adopt, that we follow them, making their positive influence part of our daily existence. But duty is much greater than ourselves. As a concert it englobes each leader in an expanding circle of concentric rings which, like the impact of his actions, radiate outward, ripple-like, to affect the world of which he is part. The ever-present danger is that, blinded by the constant concerns of coping, the leader will fail to consider the impact and requirements of his duty to the greater whole. The entire structure—leader, command, and duty—rests upon the recognition by each individual of his responsibility to the men he serves—up and down the chain of command.

And so we return to our point of departure, our home port. Leadership, with all its necessary accessories, emerges as the nicest combination of reciprocal respect and personal honor. Untouched by obsolescence, these are soundings we may safely steer by. If we would be leaders, prudent seamanship requires us to do so.

9 "BRING BACK HUMILITY"

Senior Chief Jim Murphy, USN (Ret.)

The Naval Institute was once considered an "officer's club," an accurate assessment for much of the Institute's existence. (Indeed, when I joined as a young Seaman I was admitted as an "associate member" because of my enlisted status.) But that is no longer true, and the fact that *Proceedings* is periodically privileged to have the wisdom of Senior Chief Murphy in its pages is one indication of that important sea change.

In this selection, Senior Chief Murphy reminds us of the importance of humility (and the consequences of its absence) among actual and would-be leaders.

"BRING BACK HUMILITY"

By Senior Chief Jim Murphy, USN (Ret.), U.S. Naval Institute *Proceedings* (June 2012): 14.

Headlines describing senior military officials relieved for cause are a symptom of a serious leadership problem. Far from an exclusively military issue, it extends across government agencies and to members of Congress, and every case diminishes public confidence in our nation's leadership.

Too often the "loss of confidence" leading to dismissal is rooted in personal misconduct resulting from a lack of judgment, hopefully but unlikely a one-time bad decision. In many cases the offender had feelings of being above the law, of playing by a different set of rules due to position or status. This sense of entitlement comes from a lack of humility.

The loss of humility among leaders across organizations should not be surprising. We encourage and reward self-aggrandizement and frown on those who are less self-promoting, and have removed humility from leadership curricula.

Military training used to include lessons—direct or disguised—focused on developing humility; Chief Petty Officer Initiation was a great example. More recently we've allowed political correctness and confusion between humility and humiliation to erode these valuable lessons. We do so at our own peril, creating a dearth of true humility in spite of its appeal and benefits.

Research by leadership expert and author Dr. Rich Schuttler—a former Navy chief petty officer and retired limited duty officer—has found that "humble" is one of the ten most common attributes individuals associate with effective leaders. People are drawn to humble personalities, especially among leaders. Humility conveys honesty and integrity, and makes one approachable. These characteristics are vital to leading others because they help build the confidence of peers and subordinates, thereby developing trust throughout the chain-of-command.

Still, many American subcultures associate arrogance with strength. In reality, sincere humility is the truer sign of strength. The leader who can be self-deprecating, who can cast the light off themselves and onto others, and who can make juniors feel respected, has the strength of character and confidence to be truly effective. Many leaders understand this and try to fake it. Doing so is a mistake. Pretending to be humble is worse than not being so and followers are too astute to fall for it.

Leaders are well served by staying humble regardless of position; the option is *to be* humbled, usually by a senior or in the press. One way leaders can remain (or become) humble is to consider the accomplishments of their predecessors and contemporaries. No matter how significant one's personal achievements, there is always someone who has done more.

The words of my uncle, a World War II carrier fighter pilot, in his self-published memoir *The Journal of a Lifetime*, are enlightening. He may not be a national war hero, but his combat service was nonetheless courageous and contributed directly to success in several Pacific battles. Regardless of any personal risk, hardship, or aerial achievements, former Lieutenant (junior grade) George Pleat summarized his service humbly, his closing sentence reflecting the humility of a true leader:

"One last comment, a sincere one at that: No matter what . . . accomplishments I may have experienced in the Naval Service, there were so many others that did more, suffered more and gave up more that my contributions shrink in comparison."

Regardless of rank, position, or achievement, we should all be able to name someone whose accomplishments and sacrifices exceed our own. If anyone is unable to identify at least one person meeting these criteria, it should be a cause for great personal reflection because it demonstrates a sincere lack of humility.

As quoted in *Everyday Leader Heroes*, "genuinely humble leaders build winning teams by encouraging trust and confidence." The opposite is equally true. Being humbled is character-building and better experienced in a training scenario than through failure. Eliminating focus on humility in leadership development is a mistake and contributes to many leaders' headline-grabbing failures.

Editor's Note

This article is an adaptation of Senior Chief Murphy's chapter "Humble" from *Everyday Leader Heroes* (Caboodle Books) by Rich Schuttler, published in 2012.

10 "MILITARY LEADERSHIP"

Capt E. F. Carlson, USMC

In 1937, Marine Captain Carlson—like Senior Chief Murphy—recognized the importance of humility as an essential leadership trait, but he included a number of others as well. One is reminded of the *Mediations* of Marcus Aurelius when reading this short but inspiring piece.

"MILITARY LEADERSHIP"

By Capt E. F. Carlson, USMC, U.S. Naval Institute *Proceedings* (November 1937): 1587.

When the subject of military leadership is suggested our first thought is: What do we mean by it? I like this definition: It is the art of developing, maintaining, and directing a military organization so that it is constantly ready to execute the will of the commander.

Leadership is the art of directing human beings. It is not necessarily a God-given trait, though some individuals are predisposed by environment to the practice of some of the qualities essential to leadership; and there are others who have proved that by honest effort, cheerful self-sacrifice, and careful study of human nature, the art can be acquired.

It was Napoleon who remarked that in war the spiritual is to the physical as three, or even five, to one; and so it is to psychology that we must turn if we would grasp the secrets of this art. What are the stimuli which influence the human mind and soul?

Well, there is honesty, first of all. Men like to feel that their leader is a man whom they can trust. He must be intelligent and professionally competent, for men are quick to detect the spurious leader who doesn't know his job. He must invariably be just, forceful, and courageous, for human beings respond to fairness, respect decision, and admire courage.

He must be humble in that he recognizes that fundamentally all human beings are shaped from the same mold. If he is blessed with wisdom he will be tolerant of the foibles of mankind, and be patient with individual eccentricities.

If he possesses intuition he is fortunate, indeed, for often he can anticipate the moods of his charges, and turn their thoughts into channels advantageous to the common weal. But the quality most precious to the leader is loyalty, and if he would receive it from his subordinates he must make it part of his lifeblood, practicing it in his relations with his juniors, no less than with his seniors.

He must remember that lethargy and procrastination are dominant human frailties which he must cast out forever from himself and continually check in his subordinates.

Finally, the true leader practices the precepts which he advocates. He is devoted to the interests of his men, and when campaigning with them in the field he subjects himself to the same hardships which they are required to endure.

And out of the crucible he finds that there has been forged a spiritual bond between him and his men which will enable them, collectively, to accomplish seeming miracles.

11 "LEADERSHIP: ABOVE AND BEYOND MANAGEMENT"

LCDR Robert A. Fliegel, USN

While acknowledging the existence of charisma, Commander Fliegel contends that it is an "elusive aura that is more than confidence but less than conceit." He further contends that "while we all like to think we have an adequate amount of it, most of our subordinates probably do not agree." This self-effacing discouragement ends at charisma and leaves the door open for more productive and attainable means by offering "ten nitty-gritty prerequisites for effective leadership in the Navy."

"LEADERSHIP: ABOVE AND BEYOND MANAGEMENT"

By LCDR Robert A. Fliegel, USN, U.S. Naval Institute *Proceedings* (January 1977): 72–74.

To say, as has been said, that leadership is composed of management "and something more" is to demonstrate a remarkable grasp of the obvious. What is not so obvious, however, is a definition of exactly what leadership means above and beyond management of time and resources.

That "something more" probably is a blend of charisma, competence, energy, goal orientation, and exemplary behavior. Charisma is the trait most dependent on one's inherent make-up. While we all like to think we have an adequate amount of it, most of our subordinates probably do not agree. So rather than speculate on various ways of generating that elusive aura that is more than confidence but less than conceit, it is probably more productive to look at how all of us, as potential leaders, can develop ten nitty-gritty prerequisites for effective leadership in the Navy. (Any similarity between these qualities and those usually ascribed to management is both intentional and inevitable, as leadership and management are inextricably entwined.)

Competence: Without professional competence, the most important leadership prerequisite, one cannot hope to inspire the confidence of his men. He may try to "wing it" and, if his subordinates are competent and self-motivated, he might be lucky for a time in benefiting from their output. The "lucky leader's" lack of professionalism and his need to finesse problems he doesn't understand will soon cripple him as the Peter Principle of relative incompetence takes its toll.

Consistency: "When are they going to make up their minds?" is probably the most frequently asked rhetorical question in any ship. We all know who "they" are. Continuous changes of policy or procedure frustrate the crew. Sailors and officers thrive in an atmosphere of regularity. They like to know where they stand and are happiest when the consequences of their actions are certain. Those who say "consistency is the hobgoblin of little minds" misquote the adage, for only *foolish* consistency warrants criticism. Consistency requires a thorough and well-reasoned approach to contemplated change. Poor or hasty planning results in an equally poor plan, one highly susceptible to further change and, hence, not likely to foster consistency. Experimental or strawman plans, especially when they are announced as such, are invitations to disaster. Major changes promulgated verbally, but not buttressed by formal changes to ship's directives, generally enjoy the limited success they deserve. Continuity becomes nonexistent and the institutional memory of the crew is hard-pressed to retain the current "ungarbled word" as it's passed *ad nauseum* down the chain of command.

Consistency requires a supreme effort in self-discipline. This is particularly true in the discipline area. The angry or otherwise keyed-up leader often finds it much easier to discipline his people than he does when he is in a good mood, or during those infrequent but inevitable periods of relative lethargy. His men soon feel victimized by his erratic nature; he appears whimsical, irrational, and certainly inconsistent. His rage over one man's infraction can color his attitude toward the rest of his subordinates for the remainder of the day or, perhaps, longer. The tendency to dismiss this syndrome as either human nature or as a prerogative of rank must be resisted.

A Sense of Priorities: "I don't care what Lieutenant Jones told you, my project has priority. Do it now!" So often we see "crash programs" superseding "emergency projects." To be sure, crisis management is an innate part of a military organization designed to combat crises. Common sense dictates we go to "general quarters" over urgent, unforeseen exigencies. We can, however, *reduce* the crisis atmosphere by carefully ordering the priorities and frequently reviewing those priorities. Every officer's goal should include making his priorities consonant with those of his commanding officer. (For example, while working in an exchange billet for a foreign service officer, I would send him a prioritized list of intended projects each week. At first, the lists came back reordered and lengthened. A few weeks later there were no changes; we were on the same frequency.)

Your commanding officer may view some projects as urgent for reasons known only to him (e.g., the commodore is on his back) and for one of those reasons—which you must assume valid— he doesn't care to brief you on all the "whys." A wise officer puts these items at the top of his list. Fast action will please the old man and free you to return to your original list of priorities. Any number of modifications to "management by objectives" lends itself to this approach: get your people together frequently and give them a chance to comment on a draft of your prioritized work list. Your final version should include due dates and, when appropriate, the names of action petty officers or officers.

Open Communications: As a leader first reporting aboard, by-pass the chain of command. Get all your subordinates together and give them a complete rundown on your intended policies and procedures. For the first few weeks, schedule regular meetings conducive to stimulate feedback. If you're an XO, hold separate but similar meetings with all officers, all CPOs, and all first class petty officers. Once you're confident that everyone understands your ground rules, shift gears and emphasize the traditional chain of command. Just because you find this broadcast method works (and it does), don't hesitate to make the transition.

A good example of a policy which needs wide dissemination is the one governing special request chits. As a new XO, look carefully at the current system prior to your relieving, then promulgate, *in writing*, the system that you intend to use. Define who has the authority to sign on the bottom line for each type of request (early liberty, "72s," liberty on a duty day, leave, school requests, etc.) and push responsibility as far down the chain of command as the CO will allow (e.g., CPOs approve early liberty, department heads approve leave, etc.).

Maintenance of Prerogatives: "The chief tells me he has that well in hand, XO." "Everything's in automatic, sir!" Balderdash. Many inexperienced junior officers, however, often feel intimidated by their leading petty officers who may properly construe erratic interest as harassment and make no bones about their displeasure. To be sure, the division Leadership Forum 73 officer who only talks to his chief in reaction to having been chewed out by the old man *deserves* an adverse response. On the other hand, the officer who conscientiously supervises and monitors the work of his men should not feel like an intruder; he is a professional doing his job. The junior officer *must* get involved in the work planning and scheduling details. To do so does not constitute a usurpation of senior petty officer prerogatives, quite the contrary; genuine interest and consistent involvement on the part of the young officer will serve to earn the respect of his men.

Forehandedness: This quality is often misinterpreted as a euphemism used to soften the morale-crushing effect of what the crew and many officers like to call "overkill." The refusal of many sailors to acknowledge the legitimacy of forehandedness is testimony to the fact that they don't view as important the kind of meticulous advance preparation necessary to every significant evolution. The hopeful CO who thinks the crew can get his ship under way on schedule, having set the special sea and anchor detail 15 minutes earlier, will set the detail 30 or 45 minutes early next time. Overkill? Negative. The great majority of the crew rarely feels a sense of urgency over matters it considers intrinsically unimportant (e.g., What's important about getting under way on the minute? Why is this kind of "smartness" of such overriding concern?). In short, the "hurry up and wait" syndrome is often a necessary ingredient to preparedness and is with us to stay.

Resilience: A willingness to "get burned" is part of the job. The average department head or executive officer begins his tour willing to take the necessary calculated risks that his people will, for the most part, do their jobs well without constant, detailed guidance. He is eager to promote the kind of initiative and enthusiasm which can develop only in the absence of positive control. As the weeks pass, he observes his officers making mistakes which would not have occurred had he directed their efforts more closely. Most of the errors have been minor, but he really has been burned by some. The leader now has a critical choice: he can try to protect himself against further gotchas* through positive control of the frequent offenders by never letting these "sandbag" experts get into positions where they can do him further damage; or, he can look at the situation philosophically—if he has the courage—continuing to provide advisory control but not reacting so as to quash further initiative.

The most visible example of negativism fostered by close control is often seen in the relationship between a destroyer OOD and his commanding officer. Command is such a precious trust and a make-or-break point in one's career that incumbents are obsessed not only with ship safety (as well they should be), but with the nicest points of smartness. Their concern over the latter is often detrimental to the OOD training effort since young officers usually are not permitted to witness the effect of a conning error. The CO quickly corrects all orders which would result in the ship looking less than smart. Before long, the OOD feels like a relay man for the captain and, in some cases, even shrinks from issuing commands to the helm. Should a captain modify an OOD's 15° rudder order 5° to make a 180° turn look "smarter?" If he does, he deprives his OOD of the *opportunity* to correct himself as he sees the effect of the error. Such practices not only detract from valuable training, but they also take all the sheer joy out of driving the ship.

Positive control also fosters negativism in message drafting. Granted, engineer and English majors alike have trouble adapting to navalese, that bastardized form of the language which contains our own peculiar argot, and we all need some *initial* instruction. But what does the senior, who chronically changes words, syntax, and punctuation for little reason other than to inject his own personality, achieve? Chances are that the subordinate will not put the same effort into subsequent drafts. There is no greater thrill for a junior officer than seeing a message transmitted exactly as he wrote it, and the command will visibly benefit from the drafter's pride.

Whatever your intentions, avoid dampening a subordinate's initiative. You may have to take some "hits" as a result, but that's part of your job.

Predisposition to Praise: Traditionally, naval officers become experts at finding fault. We mete out criticism, both constructive and otherwise, right and left. We're not so adept with praise except in the highly structured examples of written evaluations, advancement and award ceremonies, and letters of commendation. The first half of the old Navy adage, "praise in public, criticize in private," is usually followed only to the limited degree that the foregoing structured examples achieve the desired effect of public praise. *Look* for opportunities to give someone an informal, verbal well-done. This doesn't mean prostituting your standards in order to make yourself popular, but it does mean expressing your pleasure spontaneously and sometimes even effusively when you notice someone doing his damndest.

Criticism surely remains an important ingredient to leadership, but the "hammer" too often overshadows the "carrot." The effect of a good "chewing out" is misconstrued to be dependent on its immediacy. Seniors find it requires too much time and effort to "store up" their displeasure for later sessions when infractions can be discussed maturely and reasonably. How much easier it is to fly into a rage on the spot, notwithstanding the deleterious effect on the victim who interprets the session as public ridicule. Something is wrong with the leader who takes pride in a short temper.

Non-Attribution: "The captain says he wants this filthy compartment cleaned up before noon, so get cracking!" The officer or petty officer who just gave that order has proven himself an ineffective and, in some cases, a disloyal leader. His motives for attributing the order to the CO are revealing that:

1. he believes the order unreasonable;
2. he anticipates his subordinates will think the order unreasonable;
3. he can't stand being the bad guy;
4. he has no confidence in his leadership abilities; or
5. 1 through 4.

Whatever his reasons, the officer who always attributes distasteful orders to his superiors gains the reputation of being weak and/or in opposition to command policy. When an individual is told to get something done, he should *reinforce* the legitimacy of the order through positive implementive action. He has, in fact, an enviable opportunity to inject his own personality and behave as though he originated the order.

Threats are Counter-Productive: The only legitimate and effective threat is a suspended bust. All others fail because the leader's ability to make good on a threat is severely limited by changing circumstances. In addition, the leader who relies on threats often forgets the threats he makes, and as a result, quickly loses his credibility. Finally, a shipboard environment characterized by threatening leaders fosters low morale.

Let the axes fall without warning. This method, strengthened by reasonableness, certainty, and consistency, soon leaves no doubt in the crew members' minds that the command brooks no infractions. Some initial resentment may result as the shock waves engulf the ship, but so what? The end result is a taut ship free of the kind of bitterness and confusion so common in ships where threats are a way of life.

There is little mystery to leadership, or how one goes about becoming a leader. The qualities are apparent; all we need is the will to adopt them.

*Gotcha (got • sha). *Noun.* The sudden and volatile revelation of a discrepancy allegedly attributable to personal negligence. *Verb.* An expletive used by a senior as a preface to a tirade: "Gotcha!" A negative by-product of the accountability principle. Can be answered with "No excuse, sir," or, under particularly trying circumstances, with "*Mea culpa.*" A corollary syndrome: "chain pulling." An insidious form of ribbing supposedly designed to elicit clever repartee from the recipient. The effect, however, is usually negative; the victim feels very uncomfortable and will try his best to avoid the chain-puller in the future.

12 "PETTY OFFICERS" AND "LEADERSHIP, DISCIPLINE, AND PERSONAL RELATIONS"

(Selections from chapters 1 and 5 of *The Bluejacket's Manual*, 1st and 24th editions)

LT Ridley McLean, USN, and Thomas J. Cutler

One of the earliest and most enduring works produced by the Naval Institute was *The Bluejacket's Manual*. The first edition, written by Lieutenant Ridley McLean, appeared in 1902 and was intended "to give, in a condensed form . . . information with which every person in the naval service should be familiar." It was designed to "be of value to men just entering the service" but also delivered on its promise that "petty officers will find this book valuable for reference . . . will aid [them] in the performance of their duties, and serve as a guide in instructing the men under them."

The very first section of this pocket-sized guide provided "Hints for Petty Officers" and included the following leadership advice.

"PETTY OFFICERS"

(Selection from chapter 1 of *The Bluejacket's Manual*, 1st edition)
by LT Ridley McLean, USN (Naval Institute Press, 1902): 7–8.

Petty officers are men rated for their superior knowledge, and for their ability in handling men. They are selected for the purpose of assisting the officers of the ship to promote its efficiency in every way. They should, in virtue of their position and experience, instruct and direct those below them, in their duties, in the customs of the service, in its established routine, and in naval discipline generally.

A petty officer is not a man who is paid a larger salary because he is expected to perform extra manual labor. He is paid for his knowledge and his ability to superintend and direct the work of those placed under him. He should at all times take the same interest in the appearance, condition, and efficiency of the ship and in the performance of any duty with which he is connected as any officer on shipboard.

He should at all times be respectful and obedient to his superiors, and exact discipline and obedience from those under him. He should make himself perfectly familiar with all the duties of his rate and be prepared to fill a temporary vacancy in the next higher rate. He should be able to correctly and intelligently instruct men of low ratings in all their duties. He should at all times correct lubberly and untidy habits of other members of the crew. The direct handling and instruction of the crew falls to the petty officer, and he is clothed with the necessary authority for that purpose.

He should be an example to the other members of the crew, never forgetting that the superior knowledge and experience which he possesses, together with his manner of performing duty, and his attention to details are powerful factors in determining his influence and his ability to demand obedience.

. . . The petty officer in a division should endeavor to have the work over which he has charge thoroughly and efficiently performed—with celerity and in a ship-shape manner. He should at all times attempt to obtain man-o'-war conduct from the division. At drill he should carefully instruct his squad, or section, in the subject assigned by the division officer, making every effort to interest the men in the work, seeing that the short time of drill period is not wasted, and proceeding with the instruction of the squad or section, from drill to drill, in a systematic manner. He should recommend for extra instruction those men who were backward, or who, through a lack of desire to learn, keep the others back. In the morning watch he will, while seeing his part of the ship scrupulously cleaned, instruct his division as to the proper method of doing the work. When clothes are scrubbed, he should see that all men scrub clothes, or if not, that they start on the morning work. He should give special attention in this regard to any untidy members of the division. At brightwork, he will see all brightwork thoroughly cleaned and that oil and pomade are not left on it; this work, as far as practicable, be equally divided in the division and the brightwork of absentees should be distributed equally among men who are present.

> ### Editor's Note
> The endurance of certain leadership principles becomes apparent when reading these words written well over a century ago. Setting the example, fairness, and the importance of teaching and mentoring are recognizable themes.
>
> Compare this 1902 *Bluejacket's Manual* to a section from the Leadership chapter in the most recent (24th) edition of that same book. The tone is noticeably different, reflecting the differences between today's Sailors and those of a very different time; some may find this no improvement, while others will acknowledge the need for a less demanding, more advisory approach. But tone aside, there is much the same in the concepts offered by these two editions.

"LEADERSHIP, DISCIPLINE, AND PERSONAL RELATIONS"

(Selection from chapter 5 of *The Bluejacket's Manual*, 24th edition) by Thomas J. Cutler (Naval Institute Press, 2009): 95–98.

Principles

Because leadership is an art and not an exact science, there is no exact formula for success and it cannot be broken down into absolute rules. However, certain principles, if practiced on a consistent basis, will go a long way toward making you a good leader.

Reverse roles. This is a form of the so-called Golden Rule that appears in the culture of all civilized societies. Whenever you are dealing with subordinates, always treat them the way you would want to be treated if your roles were reversed. If you keep this principle in mind at all times, you will be well on your way to being a good leader.

Take responsibility. One of the fastest ways to lose the respect of your subordinates and undermine your leadership ability is to shirk responsibility. If you make an error, admit it. Do not try to hide your mistakes from your superiors or your subordinates. It will be very tempting to try to cover up your mistakes for fear that others will think less of you if they are revealed. This is magnified when you are in a leadership position. But very rarely does hiding a mistake work, and the damage done when you are discovered is always far greater than any damage that might occur from whatever mistake it was that you made in the first place.

Set the example. Always conduct yourself in a manner that will bring credit to yourself and will provide a model of behavior for your subordinates. Never say or imply that your subordinates should "do as I say, not as I do."

Praise in public; correct in private. When you have something good to say about your subordinates, do it so that all or many will hear. This will give added recognition to the individual(s) being praised and it will inspire others to do well in hopes of being similarly recognized. When you have to correct a subordinate, do it in privacy. Embarrassing an individual adds nothing to the learning experience, and learning is the intended purpose of correcting someone who has done something wrong.

Be consistent but not inflexible. This is a difficult principle to uphold, because there are no clear guidelines. For the most part, consistency is extremely important and should be your goal. You should try to do things in a manner that your subordinates will come to know and expect so that they do not have to second-guess you. You should most especially be consistent in your praising and correcting and in your rewards and punishments. But you must also recognize that conditions and even people change. Because everything around you is not always consistent, you must be flexible when that is what is needed. For example, you should be very consistent in expecting your subordinates to be on time for quarters every morning, but if an unexpected overnight snowfall has traffic slowed down one morning, you should not hesitate to excuse the latecomers.

Know your job. Few things are more uninspiring for subordinates than to recognize that their leader does not know her or his job. As a leader, you will earn the confidence and respect of those who work for you if you know everything you possibly can about your job. You should also strive to learn as much as you reasonably can about the jobs of your subordinates, but use this knowledge to improve your communications with subordinates, to instruct when necessary, and to monitor what they are doing. Do not use this knowledge to intrude on their work.

Do not micromanage. This ties in with the "know your job" principle. While it is important for you to assign, instruct, direct, and monitor, you should not overdo these things. Consistent with safety and efficiency, allow your subordinates to carry out their tasks in a manner that suits their abilities and preferences. People appreciate clear instructions, concerns for their safety, and suggestions for efficiency, but they rarely like having someone looking over their shoulder during the entire job, telling them each and every step to take and exactly how to do it. When giving instructions and directions, try to sort out what is important for safety and efficiency from what is merely your personal preference. This will go a long way in promoting a positive attitude when a subordinate is doing a job. He or she will feel "ownership" and a greater sense of accomplishment if allowed to put some of themselves into a project.

Practice good followership. There are several advantages to being a good follower even when you have been made a leader. First, you will never become a leader if you have not been a good follower. No one is going to recommend you for a leadership position if you have been poor at responding to the leadership of others. Second, no leader is only a leader. Every leader is also a subordinate. The chain of command discussed in chapter 1 should make that clear. And even the president, who is commander-in-chief of the armed forces and appears to be at the top of the chain of command with no superior, must answer to the American people or he or she will not long remain their leader. So it is obvious that to remain a leader, you must also be a good follower. The third and most important reason goes back to the second principle in this discussion. As a leader you must always set the example. If you are a poor follower, it will not take long for your subordinates to begin following your example and it does not take a rocket scientist to figure out where that will leave you.

Don't be one of the gang. Nearly everyone wants to be liked, and being a good leader does not mean that you cannot also be liked. There is absolutely nothing wrong with a leader having a sense of humor and showing concern for each subordinate as an individual. But it is important to avoid the temptation of being too friendly, of putting your desire to be liked above your need to accomplish the mission. Whether it's as simple as an unpleasant clean-up job or as dramatic as having to tell someone to place themselves in danger as Ensign Merdinger did at the beginning of this chapter, as a leader you are going to have to tell people to do things they do not want to do. You will not be able to do this if you have allowed yourself to be too friendly with your subordinates, to become "one of the gang."

Keep your subordinates informed. No one likes to be kept in the dark. And a person is usually better able to do a job if he or she understands why that job needs to be done and how it fits into the "big picture." For these reasons, you should keep your subordinates informed as much as possible. Sometimes, for security or other reasons, there will be things you cannot share with your subordinates. But unless these conditions exist, you should make it a common practice to give your subordinates as much information as you can about what they are doing and why they are doing it. This will improve morale and will often help them do a better job.

Editor's Note

The 24th edition of this iconic book benefits from the accumulated wisdom of many authors over the years as well as having additional space to work with (the first edition was pocket-sized and just over 300 pages, while the newest version is larger in format and more than double the number of pages). Nonetheless, when he wrote the very first *Bluejacket's Manual*, Lieutenant Ridley McLean provided one of the earliest forays into this complex subject, laying the foundation for many of the works to follow.

13 "SUCCESSFUL LEADERSHIP"
(Selection from chapter 18 of *The Naval Officer's Guide*, 12th edition)

CDR Lesa A. McComas, USN (Ret.)

Now in its twelfth edition, the *Naval Officer's Guide* has served the needs of naval officers for many decades. Like *The Bluejacket's Manual*, it provides advice on a wide variety of topics, not the least of which is leadership. In the latest edition, Commander McComas reminds neophytes—newly emerged from OCS or the Naval Academy or some other officer accession source—that no training program, no matter how good, can make one into a leader—"this is a voyage you must undertake of your own will and sustain under your own power." She offers an extensive list of qualities that officers should possess and/or strive to acquire. She wisely acknowledges that courage comes in two forms—moral and physical—and includes the seemingly antithetical but fundamentally symbiotic trait of "followership."

"SUCCESSFUL LEADERSHIP"

(Selection from chapter 18 of *The Naval Officer's Guide*, 12th edition) by CDR Lesa A. McComas, USN (Ret.) (Naval Institute Press, 2011): 224–29.

> You don't manage people; you manage things. You lead people.
> —Rear Admiral Grace Hopper

> If you want an army to fight and risk death, you've got to get up there and lead it. An army is like spaghetti. You can't push a piece of spaghetti, you've got to pull it!—General George S. Patton Jr.

In the program that prepared you for your commission, the instructors probably spent time discussing the traits of superior leaders. You may have read essays written by flag officers and been tasked with memorizing a list of leadership traits. Perhaps you wondered how such activities would ever make you into a good leader.

The answer is, they won't—at least not by themselves. Classroom study plants the seeds of knowledge so that, with practice and maturity, you will be able to train yourself to become the sort of leader you admire. No training program, however well designed, can make you into a leader. This is a voyage you must undertake of your own will and sustain under your own power.

A great leader won't necessarily have all of the traits that will be discussed in this chapter, but he or she will have put considerable effort into developing as many of them as possible.

Leadership Qualities

Knowledge. Your first requirement as a naval leader is to have a knowledge of yourself, your profession, and your ship or unit. Do you know your own strengths and weaknesses? Are you prepared to play to your strengths and compensate for or correct your weaknesses? Even John Paul Jones had his faults, but he led in such a way that his strengths overcame his weaknesses.

Do you know your profession? You can't maintain the respect of your people if you don't know your business. Your immediate goal should be to achieve journeyman-level proficiency in your chosen specialty, but beyond that, you must also develop your knowledge of the broader aspects of naval warfare.

Finally, do you know your ship or unit? Knowledge of your own command, and your responsibilities in it, are prerequisites to success in any position. Once you have such a knowledge base, you will be better able to assess any new situation that arises, make a decision, and come up with a plan of action to deal with it.

Throughout your career, never be satisfied with your current level of training or qualification or knowledge. Strive for continuous self-improvement.

Integrity. One of the Navy's core values discussed in chapter 2, integrity is the cornerstone of what Navy officers do. More than simply standing up for your beliefs, the development of integrity is an active process that begins when you identify what you believe in and determine what you are willing to sacrifice for your beliefs. If you don't know what your beliefs are, decide what you want them to be, and adopt them. If you wait until you are under duress before doing this kind of introspection, you may ultimately regret the choices you make. Set aside some time early in your career to give some thought to your values, because the decisions you make will lie at the heart of your performance as a leader.

Loyalty. Many different kinds of loyalty will be demanded of you. Your paramount loyalty, of course, lies with the oath you have taken to defend the United States and the Constitution, but you also will, and should, feel loyalty to the U.S. Navy, to your ship or unit, to your superiors in command, to your subordinates, to your shipmates, and, of course, to your family and friends.

Seniors in the Navy rightfully demand a high degree of personal loyalty from their subordinates. The so-called acid test of loyalty is the ability to pass on the order of a superior, perhaps an unpopular order with which you don't agree, and make it appear to your subordinates as if the order originated with you.

Equally important as loyalty up the chain of command to your superiors is loyalty down the chain of command to your subordinates. Look after your people, their interests, their welfare, and their careers. Such loyalty will help your subordinates build their own loyalty to you.

There will be occasions when your different loyalties will pull you in opposing directions, when you find that you cannot be loyal to a shipmate, a superior, or a friend without sacrificing your loyalty to the United States. If that is the case, your choice is clear.

Maturity. More than simply the state of being fully grown, maturity entails a sense of responsibility, of willingness to take "ownership" of a problem and see the solution through to its completion. The absence of this quality is demonstrated by someone who believes that a problem, whatever it is, will always be taken care of by someone else. This kind of attitude can be absolute poison in an organization in which individuals must rely on each other to take care of problems without being told.

Displays of temper and incidents of ridicule and verbal abuse of subordinates are signs of immaturity. This type of behavior, although it has never been condoned in the Navy, has been drawing increased scrutiny in recent years. COs have been relieved of their commands for such conduct, and junior officers have cut short otherwise promising careers.

Will. In war, it is insufficient to simply "try" to win; the only alternative to winning a battle is losing it. To have will means to not give up in the face of overwhelming obstacles, to find a way around them, over them, or through them to achieve your goal. Will means not undertaking a mission with the thought that you will do your best—it means never allowing yourself any thought but that you will succeed.

Followership. You cannot successfully lead without in turn being a successful follower of your own leaders. Your ability to do this will reinforce the followership skills of your own subordinates.

Self-Discipline. Learn to set realistic goals and hold yourself to them. From your boss's perspective, discipline is probably the most highly prized quality that you can have. You cannot impose discipline on your subordinates without first imposing it on yourself.

Confidence. In an emergency situation, your subordinates will be looking to you to be cool and confident. If you seem frightened or indecisive, or if you lack self-confidence or appear not to trust your own judgment, you will put yourself and your people at unnecessary risk. Mental rehearsals will help you learn to maintain your composure in stressful situations, as will repetition and drill.

You can't expect to have confidence in your ability to perform as a Navy officer right away—true confidence comes at least in part from knowledge and experience. Hone and practice your skills, and learn from your own mistakes as well as the mistakes of others until you are comfortable with your expertise and have learned to rely on your own judgment.

Flexibility. The need for flexibility is often mistakenly used as an excuse not to make plans, but this is the wrong approach. In order to be flexible you must not only make plans, but also backup plans, and backup plans for your backup plans. Don't become too accustomed to the status quo, and be ready to adapt without complaint when the situation changes without notice.

Endurance. Serving in the Navy can be hard work and is often both physically and mentally stressful. The sometimes extreme demands of this profession are one reason the Navy places so much emphasis on the requirement to maintain yourself in good physical condition. You can't effectively lead your people if you are exhausted and stressed out.

Decisiveness. There is a feeling among some officers that decisiveness means voicing an instant and unchanging opinion on every subject. A better name for this is stupidity.

Decisiveness means the ability to commit yourself, and your subordinates, to a course of action. Once you have announced a decision and set a plan in motion, you risk sabotaging your success every time you have to change your plans. Although you should not hesitate to reverse your decision when necessary, you should bear in mind the costs of this change and only make that change with good reason.

In peacetime you may have the luxury of taking some time to make up your mind on a possible course of action. If the matter is not urgent, and if the situation is sufficiently complex to warrant it, spend time gathering information and consulting with others before you make your final decision. Don't announce your decision until it is necessary for you to do so; this permits you to keep evaluating new information with an open mind.

Initiative. Initiative has several allied qualities: imagination, aggressiveness, and the ability to look and think ahead. Don't wait for your superiors to tell you what needs to be done. A wise old seaman once said, "Initiative is the ability to do the right thing without being told."

Justice. Endeavor to treat your subordinates with absolute fairness. Personal prejudice—against race, gender, ethnic origin, personal appearance, or other similarly irrelevant factors—has no legitimate place in a leader's decision making.

Compassion. While you must insist on loyalty, discipline, performance, and dedication, you must remember that the men and women who work for you are not always motivated by the same things that you are. Make an effort to find out what motivates your subordinates, and keep it in mind in your dealings with them.

Be considerate of your subordinates' feelings. Remember the adage "Praise in public, criticize in private." It is equally important to be considerate of the feelings of your superiors and peers.

Forcefulness. The meek may someday inherit the earth, but in the interim they are unlikely to succeed as Navy officers. You will have to learn to stand up to your peers, recalcitrant subordinates, and occasionally with your superiors to do your job effectively.

Positive Attitude. Your attitude is incredibly contagious. If you radiate negativity, everyone who works for you will radiate negativity as well, and they won't perform at their best. Be enthusiastic, and demonstrate your enthusiasm to your people at every opportunity.

Communications Skills. It is not critical for you as a junior officer to be known as a great speaker or writer. However, you must be reasonably competent in both written and oral communications, or your lack of skill will adversely affect your performance and the performance of your people. Chapter 8 discusses oral and written communications in detail.

Personal Behavior. It is not enough to behave ethically and morally; as a leader and a role model you must also be perceived as ethical and moral. Strive to set an example for your subordinates. Set the highest standard you possibly can; the standard to which you hold yourself will determine the standard you can set for your subordinates.

Courage. Courage comes in two forms, physical and moral. Physical courage is overcoming your fears to carry out your duties in a dangerous situation.

Moral courage can be even more difficult; it means having the courage of your convictions, "calling them like you see them," admitting your own mistakes, and speaking up when you feel a senior is about to make an error. Moral courage includes the ability to honestly counsel subordinates on their weaknesses, one of the hardest and most painful tasks of any leader.

Leadership Continuum Training

Although there is no substitute for leadership learned through on-the-job training (OJT), the Navy recognizes that these lessons should be augmented by formal classroom leadership training.

The Navy's Leadership Development Continuum provides progressive leadership development programs (LDP), addressing the requirements of sequential levels of leadership from initial entry through retirement. Each LDP is tailored to the needs of specific leadership positions, from leading petty officer (LPO) to commanding officer. LDPs include classroom training, e-learning, OJT, and other training events.

Officer Leadership Development courses include Division Officer Leadership, Department Head Leadership, Advanced Officer Leadership, Executive Officer Leadership, Command Leadership, and Major Command Leadership.

14 "LEADERSHIP"
(Selection from chapter 16 of *The Marine Officer's Guide,* 7th edition)

LtCol Kenneth Estes, USMC (Ret.)

The Marine equivalent of *The Naval Officer's Guide,* this book is currently in its seventh edition. As might be expected, the chapter on leadership is a significant one and, while there will be no surprise that there is overlap between this guide and the Navy equivalent, it is interesting (and worthwhile) to compare the two.

"LEADERSHIP"

(Selection from chapter 16 of *The Marine Officer's Guide*, 7th edition) by LtCol Kenneth Estes, USMC (Ret.) (Naval Institute Press, 2008): 334–50.

Service in peacetime and even more in wartime makes great demands on the mental, moral, and physical strength of the individual Marine. In battle, character traits weigh more heavily than intellectual acuity. Even in this age of highly developed technology, it is still humans who must stand the test. Hence leadership assumes extraordinary importance, for it convinces the Marine of the necessity of service and encourages faithful performance of duty. The Marine's readiness to serve and, in wartime, to risk his or her life closely relates to the integrity of the nation and the survival of its free and democratic order.

The foundations of an individual's performance as a Marine are discipline, a sense of duty, courage, self-assurance, and cooperative thinking. These qualities support the Marine as he or she endures hardships and strives to accomplish the mission. Establishing such foundations remains the salient objective of leadership. Of them, discipline plays the indispensable role in maintaining the combat power of a unit. Undisciplined behavior must be countered immediately and appropriately. In well-disciplined units, a sense of comradeship emerges and soldierly values—such as confidence and unselfishness—predominate. It is the duty of commanders at all levels to gain the trust of subordinates and establish solidarity in their units. This is accomplished primarily through the demonstration of knowledge and wisdom, example, fairness, patience, and thoughtfulness and through the administration of appropriate strictness. Most destructive to comradeship are misguided ambition, selfishness, and insincerity. A unit that has grown together into a "band of brothers" will be able to withstand severe stress.

All leaders, regardless of their fields or styles of leadership, share one characteristic—confidence, in themselves and in their cause. A person gains self-confidence by surmounting difficulties through intelligence and judgment. That confidence transmits itself to others and is a source of inspiration to Marines serving under that individual. The leader also understands the obligation to look after those in the command. The more arduous their situation, the more intensely subordinates must feel that their commanders, their leaders, are vigilant on their behalf. Again, this relates to the feeling of comradeship that should pervade a unit, holding true up, down, and across the ranks. This is one reason it is nearly always a mistake to break up a unit, particularly in combat.

In wartime, troops face enormous psychological pressures brought on by the force of the weapons being used against them, by disruption of communications and isolation from other friendly forces, and by rumors planted by the enemy. The natural fear resulting from any of these causes can escalate into unrestrained, unreasoning, and self-destructive fear—panic. All signs of panic must be nipped in the bud by the commanding officer before losing influence over the troops. But before the situation reaches a point where a commanding officer must use drastic measures to quell the first signs of panic, he or she can follow a course of action that can help prevent panic. By providing the unit with up-to-date, factual, and objective information and by reiterating that their fight is meaningful and their political and military leadership sound, the commander can psychologically equip the troops to withstand the pressures of war.

This chapter describes characteristics, techniques, and procedures that contribute to effective leadership. As you peruse these paragraphs (or any so-called text on leadership), remember that the royal road to leadership is not merely to read, but rather to *lead*.

The Marine Leader

Attributes of a Marine Leader

The young American responds quickly and readily to the exhibition of qualities of leadership on the part of his officers. Some of these qualities are industry, energy, initiative, determination, enthusiasm, firmness, kindness, justness, self-control, unselfishness, honor, and courage.

So Major General John A. Lejeune summarized the attributes of a Marine leader. Although Lejeune's list can scarcely be improved, it can be enlarged on.

The contagion of example is the central thought in General Lejeune's passage. It is not enough that you merely know a leader's qualities and not enough that you proclaim them; you must *exhibit* them. To exact discipline, you must first possess self-discipline, and to demand unsparing attention to duty, you must not spare yourself.

Much of the power of example, in turn, stems from "command presence," or the kind of military appearance you make.

Command presence is the product of dignity, military carriage, firm and unhurried speech, and self-confidence. Command presence is one useful adjunct of leadership that can be systematically cultivated. "Spit and polish" should not be confused with command presence.

Resolution and tenacity—an unfaltering determination to achieve the mission assigned to you—is the fuel of leadership.

Ability to teach and speak usually denotes an effective leader and enhances whatever latent leadership talents you possess. Cultivate this gift at every opportunity. It is a lever that can decisively influence your career.

Protection and fostering of subordinates distinguishes Marine Corps leadership. Leaders assume responsibility for their subordinates' actions (their mistakes, too) and see to it that credit is received where it is due. Leadership means looking out for your people.

Encouragement of subordinates is a tradition of Marine leadership. Give subordinates all the initiative and latitude they can handle. Encourage them in professional studies and reading. Make them seek professional schooling.

Professional competence may not make your Marines like you but will surely elicit their respect. "You can't snow the troops" is an old Marine saying. If you are professionally able, your enlisted Marines will be the first to get the word. Conversely, they will be mercilessly quick to spot a fraud. Demonstrate competence and keenness as an officer, and your Marines will be content to be led by you. Never be ashamed to be known as a "hard charger," as long as your aim is the best interest of the Corps.

Here is a classic remark by one of the Corp's hardest-charging generals, Graves B. Erskine:

> The first thing, a man should know his business. He should know his weapons, he should know the tactics for those weapons, and he should not only be qualified for the grade he is assigned to, but at least for the next higher grade.

Education contributes to professional competence. Education and study give you technical proficiency, help you think clearly, enable you to express yourself, and command respect from all.

Physical readiness, though not an end in itself, is essential for every Marine and thus doubly so for every leader. Unless you can confidently face your physical fitness test, you are not fit for active command.

The *spirit of "can-do" and "make-do"* is as old as the Corps itself. To do the best you can with what you have, to do it promptly, cheerfully, and confidently, marks you as a leader in the best traditions of the Marine Corps. The world is divided into "can-do" and "can't-do" types. Be sure you are in the former class.

Adaptability marks a seasoned Marine. As a leader, keep loose; roll with the punches. Cultivate that most admirable trait, "grace under pressure."

Devotion to the Marine Corps and its standards begets equal earnestness and devotion from subordinates. Take the Marine Corps and its time-honored ways with full seriousness, and so will your command. That is the Marine Corps attitude.

As both summary and comment on the foregoing, here is a thought-provoking list of attributes. How do you measure up?

Serious	Competent	Inventive
Disciplined	Aggressive	Austere
Loyal	Knowledgeable	Purposeful
Authoritative	Tenacious	Compassionate
Courageous	Proud	Sensitive
Tough	Resolute	

You and Your Subordinates

Dealing with Subordinates

Whether your subordinates are officers or enlisted Marines, support and back them to the hilt. They will turn to you for encouragement, guidance, and material support. Never let them down. Nothing should ever be "too much trouble" if it is needed for your outfit. Protect, shelter, and feed them before you think of your own needs.

Demand the highest standards and never let those standards be compromised. Field Marshall Erwin Rommel stated this in slightly different words:

> A commander must accustom his staff to a high tempo from the outset, and continually keep them up to it. If he once allows himself to be

satisfied with norms, or anything less than an all-out effort, he gives up the race from the starting post, and will sooner or later be taught a bitter lesson. . . .

Live, lead, and exercise command "by the book." Let this be understood by your Marines.

Keep *responsibility* centralized—in you. Decentralize *authority*. Give subordinates wide authority and discretion. Tell them what results you want, and leave the "how" to them. Never oversupervise.

Avoid overfamiliarity of manner or address. If you have feet of clay—and most humans do—overfamiliarity with subordinates is the surest way to advertise it.

Develop genuine interest in your Marines as individuals. Study each personality. Seek out background information from service records. Learn names, and address your Marines by proper names. Never let any Marine picture himself or herself as "a mere cog" in the machine. No Marine is a cog.

In your daily exercise of command, avoid the "hurry-up-and-wait" tendency that characterizes ill-run commands. That is to say, think twice before you apply pressure to speed up something if the result is simply that your people will have to stand around waiting at some further stage. Do not get them out unduly ahead of time for formations and parades, especially if every other echelon has added its few minutes of anticipation, too. And always be on time and on schedule as far as you yourself are concerned. One of the most basic rules of military courtesy is to never keep the troops waiting.

Respect the skill and experience of your NCOs. Learn from the wisdom of NCOs, but never let them snow you. Do everything in your power to enhance the skill, prestige, and authority of NCOs, except at the expense of your own prestige and authority. In public, address NCOs by name and rank. In private, you may call them by their last names only. *Never address an enlisted person by his or her first name or nickname.*

Be accessible to any subordinate who wishes to see you. It is a tradition of the Corps that any enlisted Marine who desires an interview with the commanding officer must obtain the first sergeant's permission. It is equally a tradition of the Corps that permission is unhesitatingly given unless the Marine is drunk or flagrantly out of uniform. In connection with such requests, you should give your first sergeant direct and positive instructions that he or she must report to you, the commanding officer, every complaint received from an enlisted Marine. Most of these need never come to your attention otherwise or in any official form, but this rule helps to avert trouble before it becomes serious.

Issuing and Enforcing Orders

> Promulgation of an order represents not over 10 per cent of your responsibility. The remaining 90 per cent consists in assuring through personal supervision on the ground, by yourself and your staff, proper and vigorous execution.

So wrote General George S. Patton on the subject of orders. Issuing and enforcing orders constitute one of the main functions of an officer.

Before you issue an order, ask yourself if it can be reasonably carried out. If, in the circumstances, an order cannot be executed as given, it should not be given.

Never give an unlawful order; that is, an order that contravenes law or regulations or demands that your subordinates break the rules. A good test of a lawful order is, "Could a subordinate be court-martialed for failing to comply?"

Issue as few orders as necessary. Keep them concise, clear, and unmistakable in purpose. Anything that can be misunderstood, will be.

Never contravene the orders of another officer or NCO without clear and pressing reason. If possible, make this reason evident when you countermand the order in question. If orders to you conflict, obey the last one.

When you have once given an order, be sure it is executed as you give it. Your responsibility does not end until you have assured yourself that the order has been carried out. Never shrug off half-hearted, perfunctory compliance. "If anyone in a key position appears to be expending less than the energy that could properly be demanded of him," wrote Rommel, "that man must be ruthlessly removed."

An order received from above should be passed on as your order and should be enforced as such. Never evade the onus of an unpopular directive by throwing the blame on the next higher echelon.

It cannot be too often repeated that when you issue an order, make it clear what you want done and who is to do it—but avoid telling subordinates how it is to be done. Remember the old promotion-examination question for lieutenants, in which the student is told that he or she has a ten-person working party, headed by a sergeant, and must erect a seventy-five-foot flagpole on the post parade ground. Problem—How to do it?

Every student who works out the precise calculations of stresses, tackle, and gear, no matter how accurately, is graded wrong. The desired answer is simple: The lieutenant turns to the sergeant, and says, "Sergeant, put up that flagpole."

"R.H.I.P."

As an officer, you are entitled to take precedence ahead of your juniors and all enlisted persons. This privilege is admitted in the service proverb "R.H.I.P."—"Rank has its privileges." Just when and where you "pull rank," though, is a matter of some delicacy.

Generally speaking, you should assert your privilege when your time is circumscribed by duty or when failure to do so would demean your status as a commissioned officer. For example, an officer should not waste his or her own time and the government's by falling in line behind privates in a clothing storeroom or hesitate to claim the attention of an administrative functionary hemmed in by enlisted persons. Conversely, in situations where all persons are equal, take your place with the others regardless of rank. In the mess, at the barber shop (unless there is an officer's chair), at the post exchange, or at games, avoid taking advantage of rank.

Finally, every Marine officer pulls rank in reverse when it comes to looking out for the troops. In the field, before you yourself eat, every enlisted Marine must have had a full ration. Before you take shelter, your Marines must have shelter. "There is no fatigue the soldiers go through," said Baron Friedrich von Steuben in 1779, "that the officers should not share."

Military Discipline

The Object and Nature of Discipline

Effective performance by Marines in combat is the direct result and primary object of military discipline. Discipline may be defined as prompt and willing responsiveness to orders and unhesitating compliance with regulations. Since the ultimate objective of discipline is effective performance in battle, discipline may in a very real sense spell the difference between life and death (or, more important to the Marine, between victory and defeat). It is that standard of deportment, attention to duty, example, and decent behavior that, once indoctrinated, enables Marines, alone or in groups, to accomplish their missions.

To many persons, discipline simply means punishment. In fact, discipline is a matter of people working well together and getting along well together—and, even if there be a lack of harmony among them, discipline is a means of cementing them as a fighting organization. In the Marine Corps, as in any military organization, it is necessary for people to do certain things in prescribed ways and at given times. If they do so, we say they are well disciplined.

Discipline exists in everyday life: people obey traffic lights, pay greens fees, go in through entrances and out through exits. Nevertheless, military discipline differs fundamentally from the disciplines of civilian life, because a Marine, having taken an oath to serve an allotted time, is committed to his or her duty while a civilian worker is free to quit a job at any time. For this reason, "management," a popular word in the civilian sector, is an impoverished one in military circles compared with "leadership."

The Basis of Discipline

The best discipline is self-discipline. To be really well-disciplined, a unit must be made up of individuals who are self-disciplined. In the ultimate test of combat, the leader must be able to depend on the Marines to do their duty correctly and voluntarily whether anyone is checking on them or not. If time and the situation permit, you should make known to your subordinates the reasons for a given order because this knowledge will increase the desire of your people to do the job and will enable them to do it intelligently. You must know what you want of your people, let them know, and then demand it of them.

Characteristics of Effective Discipline

Until severely tried, there is no conclusive test of discipline. Troops remain relatively undisciplined until physically and mentally exerted (a fact that shapes much of the programs of recruit and officer training). No body of troops could possibly enjoy the dust, the heat, the blistered foot, and the aching back of a road march. Nevertheless, hard road marching is a necessary and sound foundation for the discipline of combat foot troops. The rise in spirit within any unit, which is always marked when Marines rebound from a hard march or after a record day, does not come from a feeling of physical relief but from a sense of accomplishment.

Another key factor in sound discipline is consistency and firmness. You cannot wink at an infraction one day and put a person on the report for the same offense tomorrow. You must establish and make known your standards of good discipline, and be consistent, firmly consistent, every day.

Discipline imposed by fear of punishment will inevitably break down in combat or any other severe test. If you threaten your troops, discipline will also break. Discipline will not break under stress, however, if troops understand why they are enduring hardship and danger.

Praise and Reprimand

Occasions for Praise

A basic rule is to *praise in public and reprimand in private.*

Never let a praiseworthy occasion pass unmentioned. This means more than occasional back-pats. Here are ways in which you can make the most of opportunities to praise subordinates.

Promotion. When an officer is promoted (although regulations no longer so require), he or she should be sworn in at Office Hours by the senior Marine officer present. Administration of the oath adds greatly to the solemnity of the occasion and enables the officer to reaffirm the original oath taken on receiving his or her first commission. If practical, the spouse and children should be invited. All fellow officers who can be spared should attend. The officer administering the oath should always give a set of insignia to the individual being promoted—if possible, a set of his or her own insignia from an earlier rank, a gift that is always appreciated.

Enlisted promotions are effected by presentation of the individual's warrant for the next higher rank. This should be accomplished at a formation. If a parade or other formation cannot be arranged, the person should receive the warrant from the commanding officer at Office Hours, in the presence of his or her immediate commanding officer and first sergeant. If enlisted offenders are to appear at the same Office Hours, parade them in the rear, in order to give them occasion to reflect on "the other side of the coin."

Under no circumstances should a Marine be called into the company office and receive the warrant from the first sergeant or clerk. This is the wrong way and reflects directly on you if you permit such procedures.

Presentation of Decorations. The *Drill and Ceremonies Manual* describes the ceremony for presenting decorations. Even at some inconvenience to the unit, decorations—particularly those earned in combat or awarded for heroic action—should be presented with utmost formality at a parade or review, as laid down in the book. Avoid the easy solution of calling in the Marine to Office Hours and presenting the medal with a handshake. The fundamental purpose of awards is to inspire emulation. To do this, you must present medals or commendations where the maximum number of other Marines know about it.[1]

In combat, when an award can be made immediately, it is sometimes effective for a senior commander to visit the recipient at the unit, call together comrades, and give the medal on the spot. With decorations, even more than other rewards, "he gives thrice who gives quickly." As a combat leader, be alert for every deserving act, especially by an enlisted Marine. Know the criteria and Marine Corps standards for every award, and how to initiate proper recommendations. (See Section 738.)

Retirement. The honorable retirement or transfer to the Fleet Reserve of any officer or enlisted Marine should be habitually effected at a parade or review. In the case of an officer, it is also appropriate for the officers of the unit to "dine out" at a mess night, as described in Section 2203.

Completion of Correspondence Course. Any Marine who completes a Marine Corps Institute (MCI) correspondence course should receive the diploma from the commanding officer at Office Hours or formation.

Reenlistment. When a number of Marines ship over on the same day, arrange a formation in their honor. Otherwise, individuals should be shipped over at Office Hours. If practical, make this the occasion for a day off—and, if warranted and possible, there is no better moment to effect a promotion. Nothing starts a new cruise so handsomely as another chevron.

Reprimand

One basic rule of reprimand has already been stated—*do it in private.*

A second rule is found in the Marine proverb: "Never give a Marine a dollar's worth of blame without a dime's worth of praise."

And avoid collective reprimands, let alone collective punishments. Nothing so rightly infuriates an innocent person as to be unfairly included in an all-hands blast or all-hands punishment.

Before you issue reprimand or censure, be sure that an offense or dereliction of some kind has been committed. This is basic. You cannot call down a Marine just because you do not like the color of his or her eyes. Before telling off any individual, ask yourself if what that person has done, pushed to the limit, would sustain charges under any article in the *Uniform Code of Military Justice.* This can save you much embarrassment and injured innocence at the hands of sea-lawyers, while it sometimes cuts the other way to protect a subordinate against hasty rebuke when not warranted.

Know what you intend to say before you launch into reprimand. A sputtering, inconclusive rebuke only makes an officer look silly.

Avoid uncontrolled anger, profanity, or abuse. Many experienced Marines, officer and NCO, know how to valve off anger into indignation. Make this your object but at all costs avoid "acting tough."

Never make a promise or threat that you are not capable of fulfilling, or that you do not intend to fulfill. Never bluff, or you will be called in short order.

Like reward, the effectiveness of reproof is in direct proportion to its immediacy. When you spot something amiss, take corrective action at once. Never let a wrongdoing Marine slide by with the thought, "Well, he's not one of *my* troops. Let his own outfit handle it." *Every* U.S. Marine is one of *your* troops.

If you have occasion to call down a Marine not under your command, find out who the Marine is, and see that his or her commanding officer knows about it. This will be appreciated by the CO who is just as anxious as you are to have his or her Marines up to snuff. Moreover, the derelictions of an individual are the responsibility of the immediate senior. A Marine with a dirty rifle is a black eye for the squad and fire-team leader; a man in your platoon who fails to salute is a discredit to your leadership. Napoleon's dictum, "There are no bad regiments—only bad colonels," applies with equal force to fire teams, squads, platoons, companies, and battalions as well.

Office Hours

Office Hours, the Marine Corps equivalent of Captain's Mast, is the occasion when the commanding officer awards formal praise or blame, hears special requests, and awards nonjudicial punishment. Detailed treatment of Office Hours procedure and nonjudicial punishment is contained in Chapter 19.

Remember that Office Hours is a ceremony, and that much of the desired effect depends upon the manner in which it is conducted. And when you hold Office Hours, do so with the greatest respect for each person's individuality. Not only must the punishment fit the *crime*, it must fit the *person*. Never let anyone leave Office Hours with a sense of injustice or frustrated misunderstanding.

A special and important variation of Office Hours is Request Mast, an occasion set aside for individuals who may have special requests or grievances that they wish to present to the commanding officer. It is one of the responsibilities of command to keep this opportunity open to any Marine who, *in good faith*, wishes to utilize it. In holding Request Mast, one important point to remember is that the individual is entitled to complete privacy. Unless requested otherwise, you should see Marines alone, and should take all necessary steps to avoid any prejudice to their interests that might arise out of a bona fide complaint or special request.

Inspection

Inspections

Inspection is one of the most important tools of command. Throughout your Marine Corps career, you will be continually inspected or inspecting. Inspections serve two purposes: first, to enable commanding or superior officers to find out conditions within an organization; and second, to impart to an organization the standards required of it.

There are several types of inspection, varying from inspection of personnel in ranks to inspections of materiel, supplies, equipment, records, and buildings. Each inspection has a particular purpose, which the inspecting officer will keep foremost in mind. Thus it is up to you to ascertain or forecast the object of the inspection and to prepare yourself and your command accordingly. For example, if the inspection is to deal with the crew-served weapons and transportation in your unit, it does no great good to emphasize clean uniforms and haircuts at the expense of materiel upkeep. On the other hand, good-looking vehicles do not excuse greasy, worn clothing at a personnel inspection.

Preparation for Inspection

Once you know the purpose of an inspection, you must prepare your outfit. The best way to do this is by putting yourself in the inspector's shoes. Be sure your leading NCOs also understand the "why" of the inspection so that they can cooperate intelligently in getting tuned to concert pitch. Many an inspection crisis has been averted by a quick-witted, loyal NCO with a ready answer.

While your unit prepares for inspection, move about with a leading NCO, usually your police sergeant, and/or first sergeant. This enables you to see that preparations are what you want, and it reminds your people that you have direct interest in the hard work they are engaged in. It also lets you discover weak spots in good time.

Time preparation for inspection so that everything is ready about thirty minutes before the appointed hour. This gives your Marines a final opportunity to get themselves ready. It also gives you a margin to handle last-minute emergencies.

Ten minutes beforehand, have your responsible subordinates standing by their respective posts, or, if the inspection is to be in formation, have your troops paraded, steady and correct. You yourself should be either at the head of them or at the entrance to your area, poised to meet the inspecting party. As a platoon leader, you should have your platoon sergeant and guide assist you in the inspection. If you are the company commander, you should have your first sergeant and gunnery sergeant in your inspection party. The "top" should have a notebook and pencil ready to take notes. The police sergeant should have a flashlight. All rooms, compartments, sheds, and so forth should be unlocked and open. Tents should be rolled, unless the weather is foul.

When the inspecting party arrives, salute and report your unit ready for inspection. Post yourself at the left rear of the inspecting officer. Answer questions calmly and with good humor. Avoid alibis. Remember, there is only one inspector and you should take no actions or make comments yourself, except to attend the inspector. Do not reprimand your troops during inspection for shortcomings the inspection brings out. It is your outfit; the shortcomings are *yours*. Be alert for the inspecting officer's comments. These forearm you for the next inspection.

Afterward, if results have been notably good or notably poor, assemble your people and tell them about it. Give every Marine a personal stake in the success of each inspection.

Conduct of the Inspection

Nothing else can raise the standards of a command like an intelligent program of inspection, carefully followed up. Some officers unwisely discount the value of formal inspections, saying that these result in unbalanced, artificial impressions, and that COs ought to observe informally in order to find out "real" conditions. While it is certainly true that every CO must keep on the move and keep his or her eyes open, the periodic formal inspection is vital because it requires all hands to overhaul their areas of responsibility. Moreover, formal inspection is the only way to determine accurately the degree of progress being made by a unit.

Before you inspect, you, like the unit being inspected, must also make careful preparations. As an inspector, you should:

1. Know what you intend to concentrate on—in other words, the purpose of the inspection.
2. Have a planned route and sequence of inspection designed to cover the entire unit and area.
3. Organize your inspecting party. This should include one Marine to take notes, one with flashlight, plus the requisite specialist talent (such as hospital corpsman, technicians, and so forth) needed to advise and assist.
4. See that you and your party are perfectly turned out and neatly uniformed.
5. Inspections also operate in reverse.
6. Be up to date on details of maintenance and function of any materiel you are to inspect. If materiel is on the program, leaf through the appropriate technical manual, which will contain a checklist for inspection. Become familiar with the nomenclature, functioning, and maintenance indicators associated with the equipment. When you inspect, do so impartially and pleasantly. Avoid a fault-finding spirit; the object of inspections is to help and inform, not to antagonize. Praise individuals when you properly can. As you uncover defects, be sure that the responsible individuals understand what you have discovered and why it constitutes a defect. Avoid a dead level of criticism or complaint.
7. Inspect yourself. Never walk in front of another Marine to inspect at less than your best. The Marines you look at are inspected once, by you. All of them, on the other hand, inspect you as you pass down the ranks. Do not be found lacking.
8. Inspect in cadence and at attention. Have a leading NCO—sergeant major or first sergeant—precede you.

Finally, regardless of the purpose of the inspection, never overlook the individual Marine. See that he or she is smart and military. Look the Marine in the eye. Make the Marine feel that he or she is the ultimate object, and that you are deeply interested in him or her as a person and a Marine.

Inspection Follow-up

An inspection loses value if you fail to follow it up. This is the main reason for keeping careful notes on the comments of the inspecting officer.

Inspection notes should be disseminated to everyone concerned, broken down into items for corrective action, so that they can serve as a checklist. When you reinspect, review previous inspection notes as a guide for follow-up. On the receiving end, you can use past notes to prepare for future occasions. It is a grave reflection on you as a leader if the same defects continue to show up on consecutive inspections.

IG Inspections

Via the long-standing previous title, "the adjutant and inspector," the inspector general of the Corps ("the IG") can trace roots back to 1798. Today, the IG's job is to assist and examine by periodic inspections the effectiveness of Marine Corps commands in terms of ability to carry out their missions; unit leadership, economy, policies, and doctrine; work and health conditions; and discipline.

After a visit to a command by an IG team, one of three grades is awarded: satisfactory, noteworthy, and unsatisfactory. Although it may seem difficult for a unit under such searching inspection to believe, the IG is there to help: inspections are always a search for causes, not an inventory of symptoms.

Other Aspects of Leadership
Weapons Proficiency

A Marine leader has few better ways of setting the right example to his troops than by maintaining high proficiency with infantry weapons—notably, the rifle and pistol. Marines respect a good shot and an officer who is handy with small arms. Do your best each year when you go to the range. Every enlisted Marine will be watching to see how you do. Make yourself a model of marksmanship technique. Demand no special favors: behind a rifle, on the firing line, all Marines are equals. Clean and maintain your own weapon, pick up your own brass, keep your own scorebook, and keep your mouth shut.

Never violate a safety precaution. Remember the shooter's proverb: "There is no such thing as an accidental discharge."

Although you will never match your best enlisted Marines, seek knowledge and skill in firing and employing crew-served weapons, such as machine guns, assault, and antitank weapons.

Looking Out for Your Marines

In the final analysis, the essence of Marine leadership is looking out for your people.

For the sake of your unit, you must be tireless, you must be imaginative, you must be willing to shoulder responsibility. Their good must be your first preoccupation. Their interest and advancement must be always on your mind.

- Are they comfortably clothed, housed, and sheltered?
- Are they well fed?
- Are they getting their mail?
- If sick and wounded, can they rely on help?
- Are they justly treated?
- Are they trained to accomplish their mission?
- Are you available to everyone who needs counsel?
- Are you alert to help each one in his or her career?

As an officer, you demand a great deal of your Marines. But they, in fact, demand much more of you. If you let down one of your Marines, you are letting down the entire Corps.

The general must know how to get his men their rations and every other kind of stores needed in war. He must have imagination to originate plans, practical sense and energy to carry them through. He must be observant, untiring, shrewd, kindly and cruel, simple and crafty, a watchman and a robber, lavish and miserly, generous and stingy, rash and conservative. All these and many other qualities, natural and acquired, must he have. He should also, as a matter of course, know his tactics; for a disorderly mob is no more an army than a heap of building materials is a house.—Socrates

If the trumpet give an uncertain sound, who shall prepare himself to the battle?—I Corinthians 14:8

Note

1. A modified version of the awards ceremony can serve equally well for such occasions as presentation of Good Conduct Medals, civilian commendations, commissioning of meritorious NCOs as warrant officers or second lieutenants, and so on.

15 "ADVICE FOR MIDSHIPMEN"
(Selection from chapter 20 of *Career Compass*)

RADM James A. Winnefeld Sr., USN (Ret.)

Admiral Winnefeld wrote a book titled *Career Compass* primarily to provide advice to naval officers on how to have a successful career by landing career-enhancing assignments and being promoted. While this may seem less than altruistic, there is nonetheless some very good leadership advice included in these pages. This should come as no surprise—good leadership and a successful career are obviously compatible considerations.

In this selection, Admiral Winnefeld shares his practical wisdom with those officers at the far end of the spectrum of his accumulated experience—midshipmen and officer-candidates. The leadership aspects within this selection are self-evident and are compatible with much else in this Wheel Book, but one point is particularly noteworthy; acknowledging that there is frustration in having to pass on orders that are not one's own (a phenomenon that is magnified the more junior one is), Admiral Winnefeld urges mind over emotion as one means of coping, but also suggests turning the frustration into a leadership lesson by considering "how you would do things differently if you were the skipper (or that individual's boss!)."

Chapter Fifteen

"ADVICE FOR MIDSHIPMEN"

(Selection from chapter 20 of *Career Compass: Navigating through the Navy's Officer Assignment and Promotion Systems*) by RADM James A. Winnefeld Sr., USN (Ret.) (Naval Institute Press, 2005): 139–45.

> I can imagine no more rewarding a career. And any man who may be asked in this century what he did to make his life worthwhile, I think can respond with a good deal of pride and satisfaction: I served in the United States Navy. —President John F. Kennedy, August 1, 1963, to the Naval Academy plebe class of 1967

This chapter contains some additional career advice for midshipmen and other officer candidates. Some readers will have no intention of making the Navy a career. They want to serve their country, but at some point early in their naval service they plan to return to civilian life. Still, while in service, most want to perform as well as they can and be able to look back on their naval career, however brief, as President Kennedy did. They want their time to be well spent and to learn habits of performance that will stand them well in any future endeavor.

Good advice to all regardless of career intentions is to get into the habit of performing well in any job you are assigned. We are creatures of habit, and if we try to do well and expect it of ourselves, we will continue to do it regardless of our occupation. Some young officers make a mental reservation that it is not important whether they do well. All they have to do is get by, and then when they return to the "real world," they will take things more seriously. Such thinking is wrong. You need to get into the *habit* of success; shifting paradigms is not easy, and success is not assured.

It is never too early to start to gain a good professional reputation and to get into the habit of success. You Naval Academy midshipmen in particular are already embarked on making a service reputation that will see you through a full naval career. Your fellow midshipmen will quickly size you up and will duly note improvements and declines in performance over your four years at the academy. There are seven year groups—three ahead of you and three behind your class—

that will march through a naval career with most of you. Accordingly, for good or ill you already are gaining a solid basis for a service reputation.

For officers from commissioning sources other than the academy, your service reputation base starts out narrower because you have fewer midshipmen in your NROTC unit or fewer officer candidates in your class. But this disadvantage starts declining when you enter the fleet, and before too long you have caught up to your academy peers.

When I was commandant of midshipmen at the academy, I was struck by the eagerness of midshipmen to find out what it was like in the "real Navy" and to get practical advice they could put to immediate use. They did not want long lists of sterling qualities that were the sought-for objectives; they wanted to know how to do it: how to be a success as a junior officer and ultimately become a senior officer in command.

Some years ago a senior officer addressed the junior class at the academy as a group and gave them career advice. The advice was in the form of ten commandments and is applicable to all candidates for a commission.

1. *Go where the action is.* With regard to service selection, the senior officer's advice was the Navy equivalent to the Army's "marching to the sound of guns." Try to get a ship that is going to war. In peacetime select a ship that will soon be a deployer. Get into the combat forces and not support occupations. This advice was not intended to offend those going into the restricted line or staff corps (some of them go to war, too), but to tell midshipmen that our service is a war-fighting one and that success is largely determined by how good you prepare as a war fighter. You cannot always predict when a war will occur or when the action will start to heat up, but you can play the odds and go where you think the action will be.
2. *Seek to work for the best officers you can find.* This is another variable over which you do not have a great deal of control. Nevertheless, you may be surprised to find that even in an era of long training pipelines, you often have some say over what department or subunit you are

assigned to—perhaps not right after reporting aboard but later when you get your sea legs. Do not be afraid to work for "sundowners" or "iron pants" or "hard but fair" leaders. They will teach you the seagoing profession.

3. *Prepare yourself for command.* If you have read the earlier chapters of this book, you do not need any further elaboration on this point.

4. *Be the first to get qualified.* As a junior officer in any unit, you will face a succession of qualification hurdles—to get your dolphins, your surface war officer (SWO) pin, your plane commander designation, your chief engineer qualification, your department head qualification, and so on. All such qualifications take a great deal of study that you must do on your own. Look for a division officer or junior division officer billet to get early experience in leading Sailors. By the way, leading Sailors is more rewarding and more fun than leading your classmates at the academy, your NROTC unit, or OCS.

5. *Look for opportunities to educate yourself.* Your education should not stop when you get your academy or college diploma. Your professional growth will depend greatly on your ability to study on your own, to observe keenly what is going on around you, to mentally "fleet up," and to cultivate what aviators call "situational awareness." Take correspondence courses to keep your intellectual tool locker energized.

6. *Do not rest on your Naval Academy background.* Bear in mind that the senior officer was speaking to Naval Academy juniors. There is a tendency among some academy midshipmen to believe that their academy background will carry them through their early career and that extra effort is not required. The academy staff works hard to overcome that misperception. This principle applies to whatever your background. If you have prior enlisted service and graduate from OCS, you cannot rest on your prior fleet service as giving you a head start for long.

7. *Do not worry who gets the credit.* You may run into shipmates—perhaps even some bosses—who will take the credit when things go right. Do

not worry about it; the people who count will know where the truth lies, and your reputation will be enhanced if you do not jostle for the limelight.

8. *Stay as close to the operating forces as you can.* This is still good counsel for junior officers but must be tempered when applied to more senior officers. For example, senior officers cannot afford to spend more time on fleet staffs (even deploying fleet staffs) if they need a responsible job in Washington to round out their career or to prepare for such a job in a prior apprenticeship tour.

9. *Keep your sense of humor.* A naval career can be, and indeed should be, fun. Part of the makeup of most successful officers is a keen sense of humor. This is not the ability to laugh at the foibles of others but at oneself. A sense of humor adds to your perspective of proportion and balance, makes you a better shipmate, and eases you over the inevitable disappointments of a Navy career.

10. *Take all career advice (including this) with a grain of salt.* There are many roads to career success, and many think theirs is the only sure one. As a junior officer you will receive much advice. Take it seriously, but consider it in the context of the speaker's situation and other advice you receive.

I would add two more "commandments":

1. *Look out for your men and women*—but that is only half of the bargain. The other half is that they must measure up to your standards. Too many junior officers construe the first half to mean blind support for their enlisted personnel at mast, special request chits, and so on, without insisting on their performing at a level that warrants your loyalty. Your job as a leader is to set the terms of the bargain and see that the bargain is kept. Loyalty is a two-way street. One of the marks of professional officers is that they are mission oriented.

2. *You will succeed or fail as a division officer, department head, or skipper depending on your relationship with your chief petty officers.* Cultivating

a positive relationship with them, one that puts the unit first, is your most important job aside from developing competence in operating your weapons system.

Although it is not advice, you might benefit from an observation I heard from my company officer while I was a plebe at the academy. In a gathering of plebes in my company, he noted: "What it takes to make a success of a naval career is a high resistance to frustration." Frequently you will be frustrated because you are not calling the shots. You seldom do in any career–particularly as a junior officer or junior executive.[1] You must learn to handle it by using your mind rather than your emotions to guide you through the rough spots. One technique already mentioned is to rehearse in your own mind how you would do things differently if you were the skipper (or that individual's boss!).

A delusion held by some midshipmen and officer candidates is that things will be different when they get in the *real* Navy (and away from the military Mickey Mouse where they are now). Some midshipmen believe they are already junior officers and should be treated as such. And some of the people running the Navy's officer programs perpetuate that misconception by telling their charges that they *are* junior officers—and should start acting like it. Many midshipmen hear the first part of the sentence and forget the rest. Any commissioning program requires rules and regulations designed to make students qualified to receive a commission. Some rules are better than others, but together they compose a complete set. They change over time with circumstances in the service and in society, but to complain about them while you are in the process is to set a bad precedent for yourself (complaining is a carryover sport).

When you graduate from the program, your perspective will change. Let me take some time here for another sea story. The rigors of plebe year at the Naval Academy change over time, but most of those who have been through it are proud of the experience and are reluctant to see the program changed. A former commandant of midshipmen (not me), when addressing the plebe class as a group, posed this question to them: "Suppose I were to propose that we drop the rigors of plebe year—no more running to formation, no more compulsory knowledge rules, no more rigorous bracing up . . ." The cheers were deafening. Then he dropped the clincher: " . . . *but only after the end of the current plebe year!*" The groans were similarly deafening. Any rite of passage takes on a special aura with the passage of time.

Speaking of rites of passage, one in most Navy commissioning programs is what is called "service selection" or, in the case of aviation officer candidate programs, "pipeline selection" (what types of aircraft you will be trained to fly). Sometimes the structure of the program or process, your professional grades in training, or pure luck makes the decision for you. But if you do have a choice, your selection can be extremely important to your future career and how well you do in it. It deserves careful thought. Too many fledgling officers make the choice for superficial reasons, as a result of peer pressure as to what is considered glamorous, or because assignment to a particular locale appears attractive. In a recent article in an Annapolis newspaper, a midshipman was interviewed about his career choice. His response was that he was selecting a duty station near his girlfriend's home but hated to give up the chance for duty in Hawaii. Others (if they can) select a staff corps or restricted line option "because I didn't enjoy going to sea on my summer cruises." These snapshots should tell you how not to service select. For those of you who plan to go into special warfare (become SEALs), I will caution you that it is a young man's specialty. You cannot fly or be a SEAL for an entire Navy career. By the time you are a senior lieutenant commander, most of your flying or being underwater will be behind you.

Similarly in patrol aviation—an important professional specialty—you will find that most of your duty will not involve going to sea or, in many cases, close contact with other fleet units. Almost all of your career will be spent based ashore. That may suit you just fine, but it does shut down some full career options and prospects. My advice to those of you who aspire to serve in the proud ranks of patrol aviation: take every opportunity to serve with forces afloat.[2] "The focus of a Sailor's career is the sea, not just flying over or sailing under it. Your watchwords in service selection should be: sea, combat, and early responsibility.

I will offer one final piece of advice here. In the fleet, you will be serving with officers from many commissioning sources—the Naval Academy, NROTC, OCS, warrant officers, and LDOs up from the enlisted ranks. The sharp edges that are so evident to midshipmen and junior officers blur over time, and you will soon not give the commissioning source of your associates a second thought as they become shipmates and friends, colleagues, bosses, and subordinates. You will find that what counts is not a commissioning source but how well the officer performs—whether the individual is a professional. You will also find that you must compete on your own merits and that over the long run you have no built-in advantage over your running mates. You must get that advantage the old-fashioned way: you must earn it.

Notes

1. Even if you are in business for yourself in civilian life, you will complain about federal and state regulations that govern the conduct of your business. Your scope of action may be large but is nevertheless framed by others—the market, the competition, or the "feds."
2. Many fast-track patrol aviators and flight officers, during their second sea tour or sometimes in their third sea tour, are ordered to what is called a "disassociated tour." This tour, typically in a carrier, may involve service as assistant navigator or in any of a number of air or operations department billets. Most patrol (VP)-trained flag officers of my acquaintance followed this route.

16 "LEADERSHIP: THE CORE OF WHAT WE DO"

(Selection from chapter 1 of *Newly Commissioned Naval Officer's Guide*)

CDR Fred W. Kacher, USN

While *The Bluejacket's Manual* has long provided simple but sound leadership guidance aimed primarily at petty officers and aspiring seamen and apprentices, a more recent Naval Institute publication, the *Newly Commissioned Naval Officer's Guide* by Fred Kacher, targets the brand-new ensign or second lieutenant by providing a wide array of sapient advice on various useful topics. The very first chapter in this book provides beneficial advice that is intended for novice officers but has much relevance to all leaders.

"LEADERSHIP: THE CORE OF WHAT WE DO"

(Selection from chapter 1 of *Newly Commissioned Naval Officer's Guide*) by CDR Fred W. Kacher, USN (Naval Institute Press, 2009): 1–9.

Regardless of whether you have been commissioned with plans to serve as a SEAL or serve in the Supply Corps, as an officer in the U.S. Navy you will be expected to be a leader. As you begin training pipelines that are designed to equip you with the expertise and skills to perform your first duty assignment, you should never lose sight of this fact. Soon many of you will be placed in charge of Sailors who will be expecting you to provide them their course for the day and direction for their organization.

For those who have aspired to lead in the U.S. Navy, this first opportunity can be both exhilarating and a bit intimidating, but both feelings are understandable. As when you prepare before a big game or performance, it would be surprising not to feel a few butterflies before starting your first job. The good news is that you can take comfort that your training and the qualities that earned you a commission will help you to follow in the footsteps of the generations of ensigns who have gone before you.

While leaders can come in many shapes, sizes, and styles, following a few general principles will equip you well for your first year as an officer in the Navy. Whether you are in a training pipeline for quite some time after your commission or you expect to lead Sailors fairly soon after commissioning, these guidelines on leadership and personal behavior will help you succeed in the fleet.

Lead by Example

At first it may seem surprising that a new ensign will actually be expected to lead or provide an example for your more experienced troops, but that is exactly the case. In the very early stages at your first command, leading by example will largely focus on doing correct things on an individual scale, such as staying fit, wearing a good uniform, and carrying yourself in a positive but business-like manner. However, your ability to lead by example will soon expand to include a focus on operational proficiency, efficient correspondence, and a demonstrated commitment to both your command and your Sailors.

Be Early

From our very first days of school, we have been taught to be punctual, so this advice may seem obvious. The demand for you to be on time becomes much more profound when your Sailors and your chain of command are also depending on your timeliness. Just as important, your commitment to be on time signals to those who lead you and to those you will lead that you respect their time and that they should respect yours. For many of you, real-world operational requirements will depend upon you and your subordinates being ready and on time to perform your mission.

Be Yourself

Demonstrate the positive qualities that ensured your success prior to entering the Navy. Being yourself does not imply that you "let it all hang out" by advertising your weaknesses. Instead, aspire to be your "best self," in a natural and authentic manner, by working modestly on your weaknesses and playing to your strengths. Do not pretend to be something you are not. If you are naturally a bit reserved or measured, do not try to be the loud cheerleader—you will not look comfortable, and Sailors will know when you are faking it. Instead, allow yourself to grow into your role.

Command Your Organization

Whether you are leading a traditional division on a submarine or ship or managing in an office environment, your leaders and your Sailors are going to expect you to take charge. Your Sailors will want to see you making decisions, leading evolutions, and showing interest in them and their work. Some new ensigns will very quickly take to their leadership role, but you may find it a bit uncomfortable to step into this role without having gained comprehensive knowledge in your field. Although you will want to do everything you can to prepare to lead in your respective service community, you will find that, as in life, you will rarely have perfect information to make a decision or take the lead on a project. Leading in the Navy involves managing risk, dealing with unknowns, and stepping up to your leadership role as soon as you can.

Focus on War Fighting and Operational Competence

The U.S. Navy is an operational fighting force, so the majority of newly commissioned officers will be assigned to an operational job, whether it is flying an aircraft, driving a ship, or participating in ground missions. In many cases, you will quickly be expected to lead your Sailors while conducting tactical operations or efforts that support combat operations. More broadly, your Sailors may look to you for guidance and information on greater naval roles, missions, and policies, so be ready to dedicate yourself to becoming an eternal student of the naval profession.

Set the Standard

Whether you are conducting a daily cleanliness assessment of your workspaces, evaluating written reports, or leading a debrief of a tactical evolution, you will have many opportunities to signal your standards to your Sailors. Although some Sailors will always exceed your expectations, most will perform to the standards you set. If you accept untidy spaces, poorly written reports, or hastily executed drills, this is what you will continue to see. If, conversely, you professionally highlight the things you and your team need to work on and provide the team the opportunity to practice and train, you will almost certainly be rewarded with improved performance. Never walk past a problem; this will signal that you tacitly approve of the issue you ignored. Even if you are in a hurry, take a moment to point out the problem to a responsible Sailor in the space or write down the issue so you can discuss this with your senior enlisted leaders at a more opportune time.

Be Prepared to Deliver the Hard News

Whether you are debriefing your boss or providing feedback to your Sailors, leaders must have the courage to deliver the unvarnished truth. Tact and optimism are wonderful attributes; nevertheless, there will inevitably come a time when you must tell your team that their results did not match expectations, or tell your commanding officer that something is not going well. In the current age we live in, giving negative feedback is not something in vogue, but being able to constructively criticize and correct weaknesses will be necessary to move your people and your organization forward. No one wants to work for a negative leader, but providing clear, honest feedback as early as possible will prevent tougher situations in the future.

Integrity

You will be expected to choose the hard right over the easy wrong every time. Your assurance that a job has been completed or a maintenance check is satisfactory must be ironclad, and lives will depend on your commitment to do the right thing. The sea is an inherently dangerous environment, and it is no place for someone who cannot be trusted to tell the truth regardless of the consequences—your word must be your bond.

Be Courageous

For some ensigns, particularly those in the special warfare and aviation community, courage in the face of physical risks will be required on an early and regular basis. For other communities, you may be assigned rewarding but hazardous duties, such as serving maritime interception teams or on the ground in Iraq or Afghanistan, that will also challenge you to show courage. Every ensign, however, should be committed to show courage as a leader, courage as a human being, and courage to do the right thing.

Focus on Your Sailors

Although you are a new ensign, one job that starts right away is your duty to lead and care for those Sailors under your leadership. The paradigm of leading the "whole person" may seem intrusive compared to most civilian occupations where concern for employees ends when they depart their workplace. Everything from your Sailors' pay to their professional development is part of your leadership portfolio. This does not mean that you will be able to approve every special request or leave chit that crosses your desk, but it is your job to support your Sailors so they can take care of the mission. Find a way to learn each Sailor's face, rank, and last name along with his or her family situation and goals.

While learning the details of your Sailors' lives may seem difficult, divisions at sea will have a division officer's notebook that captures this information. Even if you are not in an environment where a division officer's notebook is in place or practical, there are a number of ways to ensure that you have command of the details of your Sailors' lives. Some leaders have had their Sailors fill out index cards with relevant personal information that can be reviewed easily, and now many leaders use electronic versions on computers, BlackBerries, and personal digital assistants (PDAs).

Respect and Humility Go a Long Way

Although you may outrank your enlisted personnel, you will need to respect and rely on their expertise to succeed. Put another way, talent and knowledge are not always commensurate with rank. In certain areas of naval life, your junior Sailors who are working most closely with their equipment and performing day-to-day tasks may be the most likely people to provide solutions to some of the challenges your division or office faces.

Learn to Plan

Hope is not a strategy. As you progress as a leader, planning for broader operational challenges and for the future will become a key competency. While the uninitiated might think that planning and scheduling are for naval leaders more senior than a new ensign, you will be asked to plan and lead projects or operational evolutions in fairly short order. This opportunity to plan and oversee the execution of these efforts is one of the great opportunities that make our naval profession so special. Much like professional sports coaches who prepare their team for many more hours than the actual time it takes to play the game, you will often find that your efforts to plan an evolution will far exceed the time it takes to actually carry it out.

Remembering a few basics of naval planning will help you with this endeavor. First, recognize that you will find references and examples to guide you in your planning and execution for most of the challenges you will face. Second, you will often have department heads and senior enlisted folks who will help you in the planning process. Finally, remember that planning efforts almost always take longer than you think, so start the planning process early. Ultimately, by planning with attention to detail and with ample time, you and your team will have a sense of confidence as you begin to execute your plan.

Look Forward

Great leaders, even new ones, look beyond their in-boxes. Most of your Sailors will be focused on completing the immediate tasks before them, and rightfully so. As their leader, with the help of your department head and senior enlisted leadership partner, you will be expected to think beyond the day-to-day. Whether it is creating a plan to help your Sailors get selected for promotion or creating more opportunities to hone their tactical skills, you must always be looking ahead.

Listen to Your Senior Enlisted Leadership Partners

In most working situations that young ensigns encounter, your principal leadership partner will be a chief petty officer or leading petty officer. In your first few months at your new command, these senior enlisted leaders will be particularly valuable partners. As you gain experience, these relationships will evolve with you developing confidence and making broader decisions as time progresses. This progression is healthy and expected, but work hard to maintain positive relationships with your senior enlisted leadership. This does not mean that you should always defer to these leaders, and in rare cases you may have to deal with chiefs who are not performing well, but the poorly performing chief is by far the exception, not the rule.

Be a Good Follower

In addition to being a strong leader, it is just as important for you to be a good follower. As you lead, you will execute the visions and policies of your commanding officer and your department heads, and you will support broader naval policy in general. You will often be the person who articulates these policies and directives to your Sailors.

There may be times when you will not agree with the policies or plans you are being asked to support. There is a long-standing tradition of loyal dissent in the Navy, but this dissent must end when your leaders transition from deliberating a course of action to executing this decision. Your seniors will be counting on you to bring their policies to life with honor, courage, and commitment—the Navy's core values—just as you expect from your own subordinates regarding decisions you have made. Think of being a good follower in terms of the Golden Rule—follow your leaders as you want your subordinates to follow you.

HELPFUL HINTS
What Is Expected of You—A Quick Tip

> Besides many of the obvious attributes that make a naval career so interesting and exciting, one of the benefits of working in a very mature organization is that there are usually well-articulated expectations and benchmarks to guide your performance. In this case, the fitness reports that your seniors will use to evaluate your performance include seven traits.
>
> **PROFESSIONAL EXPERTISE.**
> Professional knowledge, proficiency, and qualifications.
>
> **COMMAND OR ORGANIZATIONAL CLIMATE/EQUAL OPPORTUNITY.**
> Contributing to growth and development, human worth, community.
>
> **MILITARY BEARING/CHARACTER.**
> Appearance, conduct, physical fitness, adherence to Navy core values.
>
> **TEAMWORK.**
> Contributions toward team-building and team results.
>
> **MISSION ACCOMPLISHMENT AND INITIATIVE.**
> Taking initiative, planning/prioritizing, achieving mission.
>
> **LEADERSHIP.**
> Organizing, motivating, and developing others to accomplish goals.
>
> **TACTICAL PERFORMANCE (WARFARE-QUALIFIED OFFICERS ONLY).**
> Basic and tactical employment of weapons systems.
>
> While good fitness reports should be the by-product of great performance and not the driving force behind it, these seven attributes provide you a sense of what will be expected of you.

If the Navy Is New for You

For the prior enlisted officer who has just received a commission, the Navy's service and business culture will be familiar. For new ensigns starting their first full-time naval job after commissioning, it is worth touching on some basic tenets of naval culture that may not have been obvious from summer training and cruises. While some of these observations are not intrinsically related to the topic of leadership, understanding these cultural touchstones will help you lead more effectively:

You Are No Longer Living in a 9-to-5 World

In an unpredictable and dangerous world, it is not surprising that the Navy and the other armed services operate around the world twenty-four hours a day, seven days a week. The importance of your work and the excitement of real-world operations provide a vibrancy and variety that many career naval officers love. Operational considerations as varied as what time high tide occurs in a channel to the moonlight needed to complete a night ground mission may require that your work days begin very early or end very late relative to other professions—and those "workdays" will not always fall between Monday and Friday.

The Navy Starts Early

While the military's focus on getting an early start on the day is well known, a surprising number of new officers have struggled with the early starting times of the day—even in port. If you are on a ship, reveille usually occurs at 0600 on the weekdays, even if you are in port, and most shore commands begin their days between 0700 and 0800—still earlier than the average civilian workplace.

Timeliness Is a Core Virtue

While we discussed being punctual earlier in this chapter, it warrants additional mention for those who have not had much exposure to the Navy prior to earning their commission. Because so many more people will be counting on you to be where you need to be on time, you will find that timeliness has never been more important. It is very common in meetings around the Navy to observe those with experience arriving for a meeting five to ten minutes early and for those briefing to arrive much earlier than that. Simply put, making anyone—whether a seaman or an admiral—wait beyond a scheduled starting time of a meeting shows disrespect for his or her time.

You Are Part of a Watchstanding and Operational Culture

Whether you are working at a shore-based squadron (or office) that requires you to stand duty once a month or on a ship or submarine that requires you to stand watch several times a day, one of the Navy's universal skill sets is standing a good watch. No matter how quiet or mundane the duty, your leaders are counting on you to stand your watch or duty day professionally and with attention to detail. For young officers whose work and family experiences largely fall outside of the military, the notion of maintaining a presence in an otherwise empty building or command center outside of normal working hours may seem strange, but one of the first measures of your professional performance will likely be qualifying to stand a basic watch or duty position.

More profound than the watchstanding culture itself, you will either be directly involved in or be focused on supporting military operations. Even if your job is to track parts or file reports in support of an operation, it is important to remember what the broader mission is: delivering persistent combat power to fight and win—or prevent—our nation's wars.

Supporting Subordinates Is Defined Broadly

As a newly commissioned officer you will very likely be assigned a division officer role in providing "frontline" support for some of the Sailors under your command or at the very least in your workplace. While our greater society largely subscribes to the belief that only work-related conduct should be the concern of the employer when it comes to their employees' personal lives, the Navy takes a much broader view.

This broader view is not surprising given that the nature of our work demands that Sailors be ready to deploy on a moment's notice with protracted periods of absence from their families. Sailor's finances, educational needs, and family living arrangements—issues that would be left to employees to figure out on their own in civilian organizations—will often take up a surprising amount of your time. Like many things in life and in the Navy, an ounce of prevention often beats a pound of cure, so you will find that the very best leaders periodically check on their Sailors needs' rather than waiting for a crisis to occur.

You Will Be Running Things Faster Than You Think

In addition to serving their country, young officers most often cite early leadership opportunities as one of the most satisfying aspects of their jobs. In very short order, you will be running a watch team, leading a duty section, or overseeing an evolution at sea. Even if your first tasks are more administrative in nature, you will be expected to take the lead early, so be ready.

Read the Instructions

Whether you are preparing for a space inspection, conducting a flight deck emergency drill, or assisting in a burial at sea, you will find that there is a naval reference that will guide you in your preparation for the event and, where appropriate, its grading criteria. Even when challenges emerge that are not as specific as a training exercise, you will often find—with a little preparation and effort—that there are instructions, references, or lessons learned that can guide you in your preparation. One of the first questions you should ask yourself—and those who work for you—is "what is the reference?" because your seniors will surely be asking the same thing.

Leadership: A Universal Endeavor

Although each ensign will face a wide variety of experiences dictated by service community and individual circumstances, your role as a leader binds you together with your peers and the generations of officers who have gone before you. Your command, your Sailors, and, most importantly, your nation deserve nothing less than your very best.

17 "LEADING SAILORS"
(Selection from chapter 2 of *The Professional Naval Officer*)

RADM James A. Winnefeld Sr., USN (Ret.)

In 2006 Admiral Winnefeld wrote *The Professional Naval Officer: A Course to Steer By*. Like its predecessor, *Career Compass*, this book provides useful career advice to naval officers. While this book covers the entire officer career spectrum, the chapter dealing with division officers is particularly noteworthy and is here included in its entirety. Asserting that the Navy's basic organizational unit on board ship is the division, Admiral Winnefeld points out that the division officer is "the first commissioned officer in the Sailor's chain of command" and therefore has a pivotal role in the life of those Sailors entrusted to his or her leadership. He explains how to begin and how to sustain the special relationships that are part of this unique organization. He also has much to say about the relationship between the division officer and the division chief and concludes with a useful set of "ten commandments" for the division officer.

"LEADING SAILORS"

(Selection from chapter 2 of *The Professional Naval Officer: A Course to Steer By*) by RADM James A. Winnefeld Sr., USN (Ret.) (Naval Institute Press, 2006): 9–23.

> To deal with men is as fine an art as it is to deal with ships. Both men and ships live in an unstable element, are subject to subtle and powerful influences, and want to have their merits understood rather than their faults found out. —*Joseph Conrad*[1]

The basic unit of [Sailors] in the Navy has always been the division.[2] Depending on the size of the ship or squadron the division may number from three or four Sailors to over a hundred. The division officer (or a junior division officer, if assigned) is the first commissioned officer in the Sailor's chain of command. When you are a division officer, you are on the deck plates—and many would say in the "real world" of going to sea.[3]

Let us assume that you have reported aboard your first ship or squadron and you have been told that you will be the division officer or junior division officer for a division containing some thirty-five Sailors. If you are appointed the junior division officer, it may happen that your division officer boss is away attending a school. You are in charge. There seems to be no one about to break you in. As a midshipman or officer candidate your leadership experience has been limited to leading your fellow aspirants for a commission. Perhaps your only contact with enlisted men and women has been during a summer cruise (briefly) or with the sick bay staff during a physical examination, or with personnel specialists prior to detachment, or after reporting aboard. You may be tempted (if you have a choice in the matter) to opt for what seems to be a safer job in operations or in some administrative billet and avoid the give and take of leading others. You may argue that you can lead Sailors later after you are more comfortably situated in the command. Wrong thinking! Your best chance of getting the opportunity to exercise deck plates leadership is very early in your career. Seize the day![4]

If you do get a Sailor-leading job right off, it is not surprising that under these circumstances you feel some anxiety. You have textbook learning in leadership but little hands-on experience. Even if you have prior enlisted service, you may have some residual concern. After all, you know the mischievous games some Sailors can play with division officers who are not paying attention. As it is, much is expected of you; but you are short of the savvy that would help you over the inevitable rough spots. You look around and see that some of the petty officers in your division are older than you are—and the division chief petty officer looks downright mature. You observe that things seem to get done without a lot of shouting or the peremptory orders or drama so evident in the films that purport to portray the naval service. You want to demonstrate your leadership and establish yourself in charge, but you are smart enough to know that "coming on strong" and quickly is probably not the best move. Everyone in the division seems to know more about the job at hand than you do. Where do you start?

Getting the Ball Rolling

If you are fortunate and your unit is on the small side, your department head will have time to talk to you and your division chief together. The department head (more commonly known as a "DH") will discuss department policies and priorities with you in the chief's presence and indirectly will remind the division chief his or her proper role in bringing you along. The chief will already know this but your department head is reaffirming objectives and expectations in your and the chief's presence. Your department head will assure you his or her "door is always open" if you have any questions and will tell you not to be afraid to ask them. Questions are better than foolhardy mistakes, and so on.

When you and the chief walk out of your department head's office, a perceptive chief (and almost all are) will suggest that you go together to the division office (if there is one), or work spaces, or chief petty officer (CPO) mess to get acquainted. You have much to go over with the chief. Of that, more later. Inform the chief that you will be looking for opportunities to meet all the Sailors in the division. Avoid group introductions— or making an introductory speech to your division. Sailors hate speeches and lofty pronouncements. Speak to them as a group only when you have something important to say. For now find a place and time where you and the chief can go over the division's manning and get the chief's "take" on strengths and weaknesses if any. This process may have to be spread over several days because your chief is a busy person (or should be). The work of the division must go on and getting you up to speed is an added, though necessary, burden. Make it as light as possible. Some old pros suggest private meetings with each Sailor in order to get to know them. My recommendation is to leave that for later when you have something to say to an individual Sailor, for example, discussing a special request chit, periodic performance marks, or additional school training.

These preliminaries lead up to a most important piece of business. Have the chief accompany you through the division spaces. This tour should be set up so that you and the chief meet the petty officers in charge of each space and major piece of equipment at their shop or workstation. Don't be rushed through this process. Make eye contact with your Sailors and introduce yourself. Some of your questions will come naturally: where are you from, how long have you been aboard, are you married, what are the most frequently encountered problems with the equipment under your care, is it currently operable, who helps you with its maintenance?

Once you get started there will be plenty of questions that will occur to you. In the words of one savvy skipper this is "leadership by walking around." You get to meet your Sailors on their turf where they are infinitely more comfortable. Most Sailors these days are proud of "their stuff." If for some reason they aren't, it is best to know it early. This same old pro also advises taking aboard the fact that, "Sailors were not put on a ship to make *me* look good. *I* was put on the ship to make *them* look good."

You are doing two things in "walking around leadership." First, you are expressing personal interest in the Sailor (learn to repeat his or her name once or twice in your conversation). You are giving the Sailor a chance to size you up—and that is just as important as your sizing them up. Second, you are learning about your spaces and equipment firsthand from the Sailor whose job it is to maintain it or operate it. Those Sailors and the way they do their job are all that is standing between mission success or failure in your unit and don't you forget it. It is vital that the Sailor is informed, motivated, trained, and alert—and you have an important role in each of those four tasks.

All right, you have met your Sailors and you have seen all your spaces and equipment. Now what? The next step is for you to establish, or continue already in place, methods for meeting the division's mission and establishing your relationship with the division chief or leading petty officer. During the time you have been seeing your division's spaces and talking to your Sailors you have had a chance to size up the division chief. Now you need a private meeting with the chief to go over existing division procedures and any suggestions that individual has for needed changes. *Important: Alert the chief right from the beginning that you will have questions and that they are not intended to cast doubt on him or her or on established procedures.* Rather, your questions are a means to assist you in getting up to speed. Avoid a "grilling" atmosphere and above all don't use the occasion to demonstrate your seagoing knowledge or experience if any. Under ideal circumstances the chief should see you as an asset to the division once you get broken in. You will be able to represent the division up the chain of command and make the chief's assigned tasks easier to accomplish.

Among the most important of your questions is to determine what the chief sees as CPO decisions and what are division officer decisions. How much latitude is the chief given in the administration and operations of the division and what *must* be referred to you? What are the events and reports under the chief's cognizance that require that you be informed? This conversation is vital. Don't be afraid to take notes and pull the string on why a particular practice is accepted. Look on the chief as *your partner* in this dialog, not your opponent or subordinate. When you are done, discuss what you have learned with your department head to see if you and the division chief are on the right track.

More about Getting to Know Your Sailors

You have already met your Sailors but it is time to learn a bit more about them. This should extend to going to the personnel or ship's office and reviewing their service jackets for performance marks, disciplinary entries, special qualifications, schools attended, and so on. Your objective is to become the best informed officer in the ship or squadron on the performance and qualifications of your Sailors. If the command master chief, or the legal/disciplinary officer, or the personnel officer know more about your Sailors than you do, and you don't reverse that knowledge ratio over time, you have work to do.

The Division Chief Petty Officer

We have already discussed how Sailors are your most important resource and the key to effective performance. Now it is time to take a closer look at two individuals who play a vital role in making good things happen in your division: your division chief petty officer and your department head. We will not say much here about your department head except to point out that he or she is your boss, mentor, adviser, and teacher. The department head is not there to hold your hand, accept excuses, or even teach you the basics of the naval profession. He or she has a job to do and you do, too. But it is your job to ease the burden the department head bears. A department head needs workable solutions in even measure with the problems you identify and take up the line.

But early success in your division's performance, fostering the best in your Sailors, and ultimately in your career lies in the relationship you establish with your division chief. With few exceptions these chiefs are professionally competent, savvy, and Sailor-smart. However, in my experience too many division officers leave division matters to their chief and focus on their own watch or flying duties. In short, they see their division officer role as a collateral duty. Often they do this with the best of intentions—not interfering, maintaining the chain of command, encouraging the chief to take charge, backing them up in disciplinary matters, and so on. But don't go into automatic. You need to know almost everything that is going on and you should encourage your chief to keep you informed without getting underfoot or burdening that individual with unreasonable reporting or feedback requirements. Chiefs should see it as to their advantage to keep their division officers well informed. Fully engaged division officers should be seen from the perspective of the CPO mess as a way to head off and solve division problems and to give the chiefs the scope needed to get the division's vital work done.

Your objective is to gain the chief's respect and cooperation—a professional relationship and one you intend to reciprocate. If you see yourself as the beloved leader of children and the chief as their nanny as is so often portrayed in films about the service, you are on the wrong track. Most of the people you see in films or on television have never been in the service and haven't a clue as to how things really work on the deck plates. One of the biggest mistakes you can make is to rely on such stereotypes.

The first thing you and your chief must agree on is the primacy of the unit's and the division's mission. Today's division in the fleet is not a rest home, a coffee mess, a waiting station for transfer to the fleet reserve, or a mutual protection society. In the words of one skipper today's fleet division is incredibly vibrant, competitive, and hard charging. The division has a mission and you and your chief need to be clear on what it is and who in the division is contributing and who is not. Candor, humor, trust, and mission orientation should be the watchwords in this relationship—and each represents a two-way street.

The Weak Division Chief

So far, I have painted a comfortable picture: a capable division chief who understands his or her role and yours and is ready to help you climb in the saddle and learn and then do your job. The vast majority of chief petty officers fit this description. But suppose your chief is weak? He or she could be weak technically, or in interpersonal skills, or has simply retired in place without telling anybody. This happened early in my career, and if you are similarly unfortunate you will find that the experience will try your soul. You are confronting early in your Navy life a major leadership challenge. However, first we should observe that things might not be what they seem. A seemingly capable chief may be a "show horse" but is technically a weakling—and you will soon find out that your Sailors know it. Conversely, a seemingly weak chief may just be reserved and quiet but a technical jewel. Your first job is to find out the truth of the matter. There are other anomalies and you must ferret them out, identify them, and if needed set in motion a remedial plan of action.

With a weak chief your first order of business is to hold that individual accountable. To get the chief back in harness and pulling the wagon, he or she needs to understand that accountability for success or failure lies at his or her doorstep. Don't let the weak chief attempt to pass the buck—blaming the supply department, poor Navy technical schooling of your Sailors, poor equipment, having to provide too many extra-detail personnel, and on and on ad nauseam. This situation will require a variety of techniques to get the chief moving in the right direction. You may need the help of your department head (after all you inherited this chief) and your leading petty officers. But if you work around the weak chief you have in fact written off the key leader in the organization. Don't give up too soon. I would add that you will run into similar problems later in your career—where you must counsel, persuade, and push deficient subordinates to get them back on the team and contributing to the unit's mission. This is one of life's recurring challenges and it won't do to fire or work around the problem; you must solve it.

The chances are that your department head will already be well informed as to your chief's strengths and weaknesses. Your going over division practices and procedures with the department head gives the latter the opportunity (he or she will relish) to put you on the right path and warn you of pitfalls in dealing with the chief or others in your division. Accept this tutorial with an open mind and in good cheer. Better to get it out of the way now rather than later when more will be expected of you. A caution: your department head is not your nursemaid. After a short break-in period you are expected to solve problems and to pass only the most important ones up the line.

If the chief of your division is weak that fact will already be well known in the command and you will find that your division is already receiving extra attention from your department head and the more senior chiefs in the department. The command master chief may also do some coffee-mess butt-kicking with the laggard. But this outside supervision provides you an opportunity to get your chief to join you in running things so that outside interference is not necessary—to together reduce the joint pain level by doing things the way that meets your department head's requirements.

Your Sailors

Today's Sailors as a group are a joy to work with and lead. They are much better than they were in my day. Most old-timers are struck by the difference. Retention rates are high so you keep a lot of your good talent. These rates are so high that they would seem unbelievable to my contemporaries who experienced the societal unrest of the 1960s and 1970s that continued into the early 1980s and rippled through the Navy's ranks both on the mess decks and in the wardroom.

Today's Sailor is motivated to serve thanks to a combination of better pay, better benefits including housing and medical care, newer equipment that is better maintained than in the past, and missions that have a clear relationship to the defense of the United States. Periodic weakness in the economy on "the outside" often reinforces the Sailor's (and his family's) appreciation of the attractiveness of a service career. And today's Sailor is better led in my opinion. You have an opportunity to be a part of that improvement.

Moreover, compared to an earlier era today's Sailors are better educated—almost all have a high school diploma, many have gone on to college, and a few have graduated from college. Most have completed an arduous course of technical schooling that in some cases has required more than a year in the training pipeline. You are too close to it to see it clearly, but today's Sailors are sharper looking, trim, and wear their uniforms proudly. Well led they will do anything for you and will be proud of their ship or squadron. They are with rare exceptions drug-free and aware of the problems liquor causes in a family life and in a career. Most have left their racial and gender biases behind them—or have put them aside—and are well ahead of the general population in that regard.

With this good raw material the odds are heavy that you will succeed in your division officer duties. But you are not free of disciplinary or social problems. Your Sailors are young. The average age in your unit may be as low as twenty or less. They have all the impetuosity, susceptibility to making wrong choices, and going with the flow created by their peers as demonstrated by the youth of every generation. You will go with them to captain's mast, you will counsel them, and you will be tempted to become angry with them. What is required from you is patience, firmness, insistence on accountability, and "tough love." A few—very few—will not respond and are better discharged. Fortunately, current recruiting and retention rates permit the Navy to get rid of persistent troublemakers and screwups. But your job is to not give up too easily. The errant Sailor at one time wanted to come into the Navy. It is up to you and your chief to see what went wrong and help the Sailor return to the paths of righteousness.

Many of your young Sailors are married and have started a family. In my conversations with today's generations of division officers and department heads it is apparent that most morale and disciplinary problems are associated with the unexpected demands of family life, the prospect and fact of long separations due to overseas deployments, and making ends meet in a heavily consumer-oriented economy. You will find your counseling duties leading you into situations that you did not expect to encounter. Don't become the "lone ranger" and attempt to resolve all these issues on your own. There are a wide variety of resources available to assist in this work. Find out what they are and use them.

Most commands take special pains to welcome and then indoctrinate Sailors just reporting aboard. It starts with the ship's Web site and personal telephone calls from the command (e.g., senior petty officers in the division or the division officer) to the incoming Sailor, extends to the assignment of a sponsor, and even picking the Sailor up at the airport and providing a suitable welcome on the quarterdeck. This is not coddling, whatever unreconstructed old-timers say. It is good leadership in operation and includes getting newcomers established in their berthing compartments, walking them through their work and watch standing duties, and informing them what it takes to succeed in the new environment. If you and your chief don't see to these seemingly minor chores, you will find that your least successful Sailors will take the new Sailor in hand.

Leading Sailors and Your Performance

This chapter has focused on your duties early in your career and the central role of your Sailors in meeting your unit's mission. We mentioned earlier that you exist for your Sailors, not the other way around. Your early experience in this crucible is one of the major foundations for solid performance over a career of service. If you aren't good (or good enough) with Sailors, you will encounter a rough road in most subsequent department head jobs and in all executive officer and command jobs. Leading Sailors well and being a pro in your warfare specialty are the basic building blocks in your career.

You will return again and again in later years to the lessons learned early on in your service. Few outside your department or unit will know how well or poorly you performed these Sailor-leading duties. But you will know—and if you perform them well, they will become a basis for your self-confidence, professional competence, and pride as you go up the next rung of the career ladder. A hidden benefit is that many of your best Sailor shipmates will in future years become your lifelong friends, a bonus that in my case has carried me into my retirement years. I still hear from some of them forty and fifty years later and see them periodically at ship and squadron reunions. The experience is a treasure beyond measure.

The Division Officer's Ten Commandments

1. If you find yourself giving *direct orders* to Sailors, something is wrong. You should work toward a situation where the giving of direct orders is a rarity and justified most often only in emergencies. Giving such orders is your chief's and petty officers' job. Capt. Frederic John Walker, RN, observed, "A well-led ship's company can be recognized in any emergency by their ready and intelligent anticipation of orders and the absence of confusion and shouting."[5]
2. Just as you expect your Sailors to *meet your standards*, they will expect you to meet theirs. Their standards include fairness and not playing favorites, setting the example in what you demand of them, and orientation to the unit not your own personal benefit.
3. Job one is *getting your chief aboard* (if such is not the case when you take over) and accepting ownership of the unit's and the division's mission.
4. Demonstrate daily that you know (or are progressing rapidly toward knowing) "*your stuff.*" You should make it a point to observe closely every major

maintenance and operational procedure at least once with your responsible petty officers. This takes time but your progress will be evident to all and you will find that greater mutual respect is the payoff.

5. Keep your *emotions and your speech under control*. Steadiness is the watchword. Better too few words than too many. Avoid lavishness in praise and excesses in criticism.
6. *Beware the Sailor who attempts to end-run the chief* or his or her petty officers. Your first question should be: Who is your leading petty officer and does he or she know this? If not, why not? Don't accept quibbles or excuses in their answers.
7. Insist on *accountability*. There is a chain of accountability in your division from top to bottom. Someone is to blame or to be credited when things go wrong or right. Good intentions are never a sufficient explanation. Find the source of the problem and then fix it.
8. *Avoid a myopic focus on your own job*. Look up to your department head and out to other divisions and departments to see how all the pieces fit. This is not only the pathway to professional growth but also will help you keep the work of your division in perspective. Seeing the big picture means seeing the forest *and* the trees at the same time.
9. *Loyalty is a two-way street*. Just as you must earn the respect of your Sailors, they must earn yours by their performance. When you back up your Sailors it is a token of respect that they have earned whether it is for a good performance evaluation or a recommendation for leniency at mast.
10. The *example* you set is important. Your uniform, your demeanor, your focus on the unit's mission, and your diligence set the tone for your division. Your Sailors, in ways you will not understand, will watch your every move and will be the first to detect a false note.

We began this chapter with a quote from Joseph Conrad and so we shall end it. "It is the captain who puts the ship ashore; it is *we* who got her off."[6] Your good judgment and your bluejackets are all that stand between you and failure.

Notes

1. Joseph Conrad. *A Personal Record and a Mirror of the Sea* (London: Penguin, 1998), 158.
2. *Ship's Organization and Personnel* (Annapolis, Maryland: Naval Institute Press, 1972), 27.
3. See Rear Adm. James G. Stavridis, USN, and Cdr. Robert Girrier, USN. *Division Officer's Guide*, 11th ed. (Annapolis, Maryland: Naval Institute Press, 2004). This book is the definitive treatment of the division officer's duties.
4. For an additional source of good advice on how to conduct yourself on reporting aboard your first duty station, see Lt. Cdr. Fred W. Kacher, USN, "New Guy 101: Your First Tour of Duty," U.S. Naval Institute *Proceedings* (June 2004): 72–73. Reprinted in appendix B.
5. Terrence Robertson. *Escort Commander: Captain Frederic John Walker, The Man Who Helped Free the Atlantic of the U-Boat Menace* (1956; repr., New York: Nelson Doubleday, 1979), 75.
6. Conrad, *A Personal Record*, 194.

18 "THE TUNED-IN LEADER"

ENS Robert Van Winter, USN

Like the previous selection, this essay focuses on the division officer. Every year, *Proceedings* publishes the winners of the Commander William Earl Fannin, [Naval Academy] Class of 1945 Capstone Essay Contest. These essays are written by Naval Academy midshipmen in their first-class (senior) year and subsequently published after their commissioning. Ensign Van Winter makes up for his limited experience by relying upon the wisdom passed on to him by his father who served in the Navy as an enlisted man in the early 1970s. Recognizing that his primary responsibility is "to do everything in your power to ensure that your ship is able to complete her mission," he contends that this is best accomplished when the division officer recognizes that besides ensuring the professional development of the Sailors in his or her charge, he/she must also ensure that "they have a healthy life in regard to their families, finances, and living situations."

"THE TUNED-IN LEADER"

By ENS Robert Van Winter, USN, U.S. Naval Institute *Proceedings* (June 2013): 68–72.

The ability to serve as an officer in the U.S. Navy is an honor unmatched by any other. You have the ability not only to serve your country, but to influence positively the lives of the people placed within your care. As a division officer you are responsible for those in your division. Beyond their professional development and accession through the ranks, you are obligated to make sure that they have a healthy life in regard to their families, finances, and living situations. You are increasingly required to assure their well-being under way and to do everything within your power to return them safely to their families ashore. This means that you must strive to create as safe an environment as possible and to ensure that all the members of your division are able to do their jobs.

Lead and Learn

As a surface warfare officer, you are a leader of sailors from the second you are commissioned. While it is essential that you are able to stand watch and perform the duties required of you on the ship, the most important part of the division officer's job is to lead ably and support the sailors within your division. In this sense, the greatest asset you have is the senior enlisted leader of your division. Your chief or senior chief along with your first-class petty officer are important resources who not only know the best ways to handle your division, but who are experienced hands skilled at their jobs. Behind every great commanding officer is a chief who molded and shaped him or her as a young junior officer. The senior enlisted are the backbone of the Navy and the officer corps.

Beyond the ship, you must help your sailors be safe and secure within their homes and their marriages. The division officer must be a resource to help them find financial, marriage, and child-raising guidance. It is also essential to have a working knowledge of these subjects so that you are able to provide basic counseling. Many times as an ensign and lieutenant, junior grade, and potentially even later in your career, you will be incredibly inexperienced in these areas.

Often, the sailors coming to you will be older and have more life experience. As an officer, however, you must have the right answer, and it is your job to advise them knowledgeably.

In order to be focused on the safety, security, and happiness of your sailors, it is essential that you are vigilant and observant. You must know your people on a personal level so that you can notice changes in their affect or demeanor. You should be vigilant always, but some of the most important times are the months leading up to and immediately following deployment. Traditionally, these are the times in which service members find themselves in the most trouble. Whether due to leaving family at home, the stress of going to sea again after multiple deployments, or the anxiety of leaving behind financial troubles, the days leading up to deployment can be stressful beyond the inspections, preparatory under ways, and exercises. It is essential that as a division officer you make this period as easy as possible for your sailors who may be having problems with these stressors.

The same can be said as the ship returns from deployment. The sailors may be worried about coming home to financial troubles, a difficult family situation, or the unknown. If sailors are worried about their problems away from the ship they will not be focused on the tasks at hand and will become ineffective and even dangerous in their jobs. This is the greatest reason to be observant of those in your division. You must be sure that they are not distracted by issues away from the ship (or even on the ship) that would cause them to be less effective at their job and therefore a greater safety hazard.

A warship is a dangerous place to work, and a distracted sailor unfocused on the task at hand greatly increases the risk of accidents and mistakes. These mistakes could cause serious problems for crew who fall victim to a resulting casualty. This must be avoided at all cost; therefore, it is essential that you are familiar with the personalities of the sailors within your division.

Dangers of Distraction

During a summer cruise I learned firsthand just how dangerous a distracted sailor can be. A sailor was having trouble with his girlfriend at home and was not getting much sleep. As such, his job suffered, and he let standards slip. This continued for some time. Neither his chief nor his division officer came to him to help fix his issues, yet they noticed his work ethic and effectiveness sliding. The final straw came when it was discovered that he had been gundecking the maintenance log book for the torpedo room, for which he had been responsible. Because he had been gundecking the log book, there was an issue with one of the watertight doors, allowing some sea water to flow in. This became serious when the water began to leak into the torpedo room, and an enlisted sailor in charge of the torpdeo room's maintenance noticed. This is a serious risk because torpedoes are activated by seawater. If the torpedoes had not been elevated on shelves—remaining dry—they could have been set off and potentially destroyed the ship.

The sailor went to Captain's Mast and was punished heavily. Both the ship and her crew were lucky that the ship had not been destroyed by an explosion resulting from the torpedoes coming into contact with salt water. Worse, had the ship faced a casualty and the room flooded, even if the flood was able to be contained to a few spaces around the torpedo room, the issue with the watertight doors would have caused a massive explosion when the room flooded and all of the ship's torpedoes exploded. This entire incident could have been avoided had either the division officer or the chief taken the time to talk with the sailor and asked him about any issues that he was having in his personal life.

This is a lesson in caring about sailors as people. If the time is taken to do so, then many problems that become larger issues in the division and on the ship can be avoided. It is a simple fix: All you must do is roll up your sleeves, step back from your computer, and make sure you know your people, learn their jobs, and find out what ways you can help them improve as individuals and sailors. In doing so, you may find that there are many important lessons that you can take away from your sailors and apply to your own life and career.

Lead and Serve

As the son of a former enlisted sailor, I have an appreciation for the problems junior enlisted sailors face. My father served on board a destroyer in the late

1970s and left the Navy for college as a third-class petty officer operations specialist. The stories about his years in the Navy taught me not only to appreciate the difficulties of the junior enlisted sailors, but also to recognize the importance of senior enlisted leaders to the Navy as a whole and the junior officer corps specifically. While the senior enlisted are the backbone of the Navy, the majority of the work is done by the junior enlisted sailors. Responsibility is given to the lowest possible level at which it can still be feasibly expected that the member is competent enough to be held responsible for their decisions. This process is beneficial to the officers and senior enlisted because it allows them to teach leadership to the youngest members of the crew in increments. This is the heart and soul of your job as a division officer: You not only must be a leader immediately, but you must also teach other people who may be your age or older how to be leaders. These sailors may have never led in their lives, but you must find ways to make them leaders. This challenge will be your greatest as a young division officer, but it will also be your most rewarding.

The best way to instill an attitude of excellence throughout the ship is to establish a sense of pride in one's work and find ways to reward hard work and effort. A good way to create an environment that fosters these habits is by doing everything in your power to give your enlisted sailors the opportunity to work on their own career advancement. Whether this is extra time laid out for them to study for exams, extra work put in by the division officer or the chief on evaluations, or medals and citations for achievements, by showing that as the division officer you care about the members of your crew, you strive to create an environment that benefits the entire ship. This will also help your chief because a division with a strong work ethic that performs well and continually thrives reflects positively on the leadership of your chief, helping his/her own advancement and career opportunities.

Evaluations are an opportunity for the division officer to help repay the chief for the hard work of molding a young officer and helping him/her navigate the minefield of that first tour. One of the best ways for a young officer to help is by taking some of the administrative burden off the chief's hands, allowing the chief to go home instead of spending long nights on the ship. As a young and perhaps unmarried officer, you are able to help your chief maintain a good work/life balance. Improving the family life of your chief instills him/her with more energy to focus on the ship, which in turn improves your division because the chief has the energy to better help the sailors. By helping your sailors to the best of your ability, you can improve your division and in turn help yourself by creating successful sailors; such sailors have fewer disciplinary issues, which reduces unnecessary paperwork for you. This servant leadership is the essence of the military and is the defining characteristic of your job as a surface warfare officer.

Surface warfare and the officers and enlisted serving on board warships are both the backbone and the earliest identity of the U.S. Navy. Before there were SEALs, pilots, EOD technicians, Marines, or any other branch of the Navy, there were surface warriors. The Navy was formed to protect American shipping interests in the Mediterranean as they came under attack by North African pirates. Under Thomas Jefferson, ships were given letters of marque and reprisal in order to go after the pirates and protect American interests. Today, we face many of the same challenges off the coast of Africa as we fight to protect shipping lanes and ensure the safe passage and freedom of navigation for all.

As a division officer on board an American warship, it is your job to do everything in your power to ensure that your ship is able to complete her mission. This means it is your duty to find every way possible to protect and support your sailors. As the global force for good in the world, America is responsible for the 70 percent of the Earth covered by water, the 80 percent of the Earth's population who live near water, and the 90 percent of the world's trade that crosses the oceans' shipping lines. For that reason, the U.S. Navy remains, and must always be, 100 percent on watch.

19 "SO YOU WANT TO BE A DEPARTMENT HEAD"

LCDR Fred W. Kacher, USN

One of the key leadership positions in the Navy is the department head. Success in this role usually leads to the opportunity to become an executive officer, the last stepping stone to command. While Commander Kacher's article offers advice beyond that of simple leadership, there is an underlying message that makes the correlation between leadership and the successful department head tour apparent and indispensable.

"SO YOU WANT TO BE A DEPARTMENT HEAD"

By LCDR Fred W. Kacher, USN, U.S. Naval Institute *Proceedings* (August 2002): 71–73.

Surface warriors aspire to command ships, not serve as department heads. Department heads are sometimes viewed as the Navy's middle managers, a prejudice with consequences that do not serve the Navy well. First, the job's reputation drives some great young leaders to look for challenges beyond the Navy. Second, this attitude undervalues the tour, which provides commanding officers their longest and most substantive at-sea leadership opportunity prior to taking command. From my conversations with aviators and submariners, I sense that these middle-management perceptions persist in other line communities as well.

However, when I talk to department heads who recently have completed their tours, their memories run counter to the stereotype of the department head as the put-upon middle manager. Hard work was a mainstay (no surprise), but so were camaraderie, satisfaction, and even fun. From these conversations some indispensable advice emerged that, although it focuses on aspiring surface-warfare department heads, could apply to all professional naval leaders. I hope these tips will help those considering taking the department-head plunge not only to survive but also to thrive in this critical at-sea billet.

Strengthen Your Weaknesses Early

. . . as in before you arrive on your ship. Use Department Head School for what it is, the last "free" opportunity you will enjoy to gain knowledge before reporting. The instructors, almost all screened executive officers, have been detailed there based on their expertise. Don't just play to your strengths—if you are an air warfare junkie, stand as tactical action officer (TAO) in the undersea warfare simulator. Use the simulators to flex ship-handling skills that have not been exercised during your shore tour. Think about the things that, as a division officer, you did not worry about because they were "department-head issues." For me, supply management, departmental budgeting, and combat system maintenance programs warranted extra attention.

Be Ready to Sit in the Chair

Because you almost always will be relieving a fully qualified TAO, your ship will be looking for you to step up as soon as you can. Whether you are TAO-qualified or not, the watch team requirements of the training cycle almost immediately demand your insertion as the TAO of the future. The members of your chain of command will understand that you will not be in midseason form when you arrive, but neither will they expect you to be clueless. Start preparing now.

Command Your Department
You likely will be the leader of almost 100 officers and sailors on a U.S. Navy ship. Carry yourself that way. Find opportunities to address your troops, set your agenda, and be a leader. I have yet to meet a commanding officer (CO) or executive officer (XO) who wants to go back and do a third department-head tour; make sure you leave them no doubt that you are on the job.

Win the Battle of Information Warfare
. . . and you never will lose the war. Whether you are dealing with afloat training group assessors, squadron representatives, or contractors during a yard period, work to "out-knowledge" the experts. These efforts, which include walking your spaces, visiting technical representatives, and reading the fine print, will help to ensure your team drives the program rather than the reverse. Demand from your subordinates concise, honest reports that allow you to solve the problem before it is too late. Honor your CO and XO with the same courtesy.

Extend Your Planning Horizon
A division officer who looks a month in advance might be exceptional; a department head who looks only that far will be a failure. Recognize right away that almost every substantial challenge, inspection, or exercise will take at least two months to plan and execute. Consider mapping a 90-day campaign, day by day, to meet every broad requirement for the quarter beyond the one you are in. Develop a detailed roadmap of the ship's schedule for the next year as well. In addition, develop an event preparation matrix for every major challenge and warfare area to ensure that your sailors are set up to succeed. When emerging events disrupt your preparations, these plans provide the foundation to adapt to changing circumstances.

Don't Just Answer the Mail
The routine demands of message traffic, reports, evaluations, and awards packages often will be enough to fill the workday. To borrow a phrase from one of my favorite division officers, take the time to "dream big" rather than being defined by your in-box.

Demand and Deliver All-but-the-Signature Staff Work

Although you do not want to be defined by your in-box, the quality of what leaves that in-box matters. Like the old adage that a ship often is judged by its communications, a department often is judged by its staff work. Demanding complete work from your subordinates does not mean that you can sign a fitness report, message, or firing plan without reading it, but it establishes a standard that will signal your expectations and prevent you from doing the work that your division leaders are there to do. In addition, providing your boss the most complete product possible saves time by preventing rewrites. Your "perfect" effort may fall short under the XO's scrutiny, but imagine how much greater these shortfalls would be had you dedicated only 80% of the attention to detail you were capable of giving.

Focus on War Fighting

Remind your folks that everything we do is a means to one end: combat capability. The terrible events of 11 September 2001 reminded all of us to focus on the basics; focus on the war fighter in your span of control as well. Seek out opportunities for your department to fight fires, run air defense drills, or hone whatever combat competency is its core responsibility. As the primary scheduling force in your department, put combat drills on the calendar first rather than trying to jam them in as an afterthought.

Manage Your Equipment

During my tenure I never pretended to be the equipment expert, but I made sure I could expertly articulate our equipment management strategy. Monitor your technicians, other ships, and shore experts to anticipate high-failure items, order needed parts, and find opportunities to groom your systems. Former General Electric Chairman Jack Welch's admonition to his managers, "Don't Walter Cronkite me," reminds us that our job is not merely to bring the CO the bad news of our latest casualties, but to provide options for how to fix them as well. Make sure your eight o'clock reports completely and accurately capture the problem-solving spirit for which you want your department to be known.

Realize Division Officers Are Executive Talent

My number-one joy as a department head was leading some of the finest young Americans in our country. By nature of their profession they are idealists who want to be inspired. Treat your division officers like the frontline Fortune 500 executive talent they are. (Consider all the division officers who are accepted to top-ten business schools every year.) Make sure they understand that, as your frontline leaders and managers, they not only will run a division, but they also will be war fighters and will tackle departmental challenges.

If you plan on demanding the best from them, make sure they are afforded the best equipment, loyalty, treatment, and leadership possible; they will not disappoint you. Finally, avoid impressing your division officers with how much harder you work than they do. Let them see you enjoy your job, grab a workout, or laugh during a departmental dinner. If they think you don't like your job, how are you going to convince them to come back to sea and relieve you?

Count on Your Senior Enlisted

You cannot afford to go it alone. With division officers rotating fairly quickly, your more permanent partnerships may well be with your chiefs. Treat your departmental chief petty officer as the command master chief (CMC) of your department. My departmental leading chief petty officer made the things that can drive department heads crazy—berthing inspections, enlisted rankings, working parties—"fire and forget" items. Your departmental "CMC" will do the same for you.

Never Forget Your Sailors

Every interaction with a sailor is a leadership opportunity. Seek out the stars in your department and push them for every commissioning program available. This effort not only demonstrates that you recognize truly noteworthy performances, but it also provides your best with the upward mobility that is part of the American Way. A word of advice: don't yell at your sailors. While there are exceptions to every rule (for example, safety and combat situations), the image of a senior manager dressing down a young blue shirt in public is not what our business is about. Your division officers and chiefs will address whatever transgression you have witnessed after you let them know about it.

Follow Up

I recently asked a Marine serving on his first ship the differences in leadership between the Navy and Marine Corps. He answered, "Marines follow up." He explained that Navy leaders, based on their faith in their people, often would issue an order and would not check on its progress until just before completion. "Follow up" encapsulates what department heads must do best. We check our folks' progress, reassess, provide guidance and correction, and bear the lion's share of the credit for their labors. As I look back on the adventures and misadventures a department head can face, I believe that bumper stickers with the words *Follow up* should be attached to every car in fleet parking!

There are many people who view their department-head tours as the best of times and the worst of times. The job is hard work; few things worth doing come without it. But these tours are satisfying as well. There is no better way to describe meeting Tomahawk tasking on time and on target, commissioning great sailors, and serving on the USS *Princeton* (CG-59), which distinguished herself in support of Operation Enduring Freedom. These tips might help convince our best and brightest that a successful department-head ride is in their future.

20 "ON LEADING SNIPES"

LT Jim Stavridis, USN

Long before he was Supreme Allied Commander for Global Operations at NATO, Jim Stavridis was a department head. Like most chief engineers, he found the challenges of leading the Sailors below decks a unique challenge. Unlike most chief engineers, he found time to share the wisdom gleaned from his experiences by writing about it! Here we find sound advice from one of the U.S. Navy's most interesting (and amazing) officers.

"ON LEADING SNIPES"

By LT Jim Stavridis, USN, U.S. Naval Institute *Proceedings* (January 1981): 74–76.

It is a different world there, seven decks down, a world where the temperatures routinely soar over the 130° mark, where a watchstander can trace his rounds in his own sweat on greasy deckplates. The fireroom and engine-room are the universe set aflame, a burlesque vision of fire and heat and noise and swift, dark machines that whine and turn and spin throughout the long at-sea periods. Many of the ships are more than 20 years old—merely replacing parts to some of the original equipment can require having to deal with defunct companies and retired technical representatives. The combined deficiency lists would take years to correct, if all the ship did was remain lashed to the pier with full shipyard support. The manning is wretchedly low, with watchstanders often on 6-on/6-off shift work, in a place where all the vitality and energy are drained from a man within the first hour in the space because of the heat and noise. Retention is low—with machinist's mates and boiler technicians (BTs) the most critical of ratings.

The enlisted men who work here face all this and worse. For a deployment, their liberty will probably expire a full 48 hours before the ship gets under way. For the week prior, they will be lit-off, standing their 6-on/6-off, or 8 and 16 if they are lucky, beaten down by the work load and the personnel qualification standards (PQS) and the planned maintenance system (PMS) and leak lists and lagging lists and the equipment deficiency lists and operating logs and all the rest. They are men who are expected to sweat their hours away in the "pit" on watch, then follow with a regular working day. Everything they do must be done professionally and expertly, for the operating logs do not lie, revealing as they do the missed soundings and the bad surface blows and every other mistake and miscue. It seems at times a load so heavy as to shut out totally the mythical light at the end of the tunnel.

Personnel retention here is so low, because the only light most of them *can* see is the one that illuminates a way out of the Navy. Most of the machinist's mates joined thinking they would work lathes and presses, not main engines, and the BTs enter the fold with even less understanding of what they will be doing. They remain usually forgotten and unnamed until the brightness of a Class Bravo Fire or the darkness of the load suddenly dropped brings them smartly into focus.

Someone has to lead them. And in every plant, on both coasts, there are some officers who can lead a snipe and others who cannot. For some engineer officers, the men in the holes are willing to work 16-, 18-, to 20-hour days, going port and starboard on duty days to prepare for an operational propulsion plant exam (OPPE).

Other engineers cannot light off a plant without a virtual strike. Certain ships, with good, snipe-capable officers, can make commitments, win "E"s, steam the plant, tour the VIPs, and all the rest. Others struggle to turn a shaft, draw a vacuum, or line up a low pressure drain tank. The key is *snipe leadership*, or the presence in the engineering department of what could be called snipe-capable officers.

There are several key attributes that the snipe-capable officer possesses. The first is some training in the technical areas. This does not necessarily mean he must be a mechanical engineer. The officer might have been an English or a psychology major—but he must at least have taken some math and engineering science, have some understanding of propulsion, and maybe even have an awareness of thermodynamics and electrical engineering. He should know what a spanner wrench and a tap and die set are, and perhaps even have used them at some time. He ought to have some idea of what a working man is capable of doing in what length of time. These are all attributes that come with the basic background training package. An officer who does not have any of these essential background items should not be ordered into a snipe-capable officer's billet.

The second key asset for the snipe-capable officer is that he be able to obtain the respect of his men. This does not mean he needs to be a macho, drinking, run-with-the-pack individual. But coupled with the technical knowledge there should be a tough, pragmatic approach to life. Being able to mix well with the enlisted men from a bantering, give-and-take conversational standpoint to being able to throw the football around with them at the division party all count in gaining respect. Snipes, generally, are physical, and the men they find easiest to respect and, thus follow, mirror these qualities.

Training in the plant to which he is detailed is a third background item that can make an officer more snipe-capable. The ability to walk into a plant and have a conversation about the locations of the equipment, their Outputs and parameters, and the idiosyncrasies of the plant is important. This coupled with the ability to ask any question without feeling or appearing stupid, but in a natural, curious way, can take an officer a long way into the ranks of the snipe-capable.

The leadership approach taken—that combination of charisma and dedication and style that makes it possible to ask men to do the hardest, dirtiest work on the ship—is just as important as the officer's background. The basic primer of snipe leadership is simply *deckplate leadership*. No engineer has ever had a department or steamed a plant from the log room. It is not possible. The engineer officer must exhibit a sure, steady presence in the spaces his people work. They must see him sweat next to them. He must have dirty hands and coveralls and a rag in his pocket. All the excellent hearing conservation programs will fall to nothing if the troops do not see the engineer officer and his officers in the spaces wearing their hearing protection and enforcing the program. Heat stress programs tend to lose all impact when administered from the air-conditioned cocoon of a log room or a central control. One pair of hands made greasy holding a recently pulled valve is worth a thousand memoranda to the main propulsion assistant (MPA) about maintenance actions.

Second, the engineer officer must establish a strict set of standards and enforce them. These are standards of professionalism and watchstanding that are general throughout the plant and in addition to the use of the engineering operational sequence system, instructions, standing orders, night orders, etc. What is required here is not a paperwork policy, but rather an attitude instilled in the people that says, "Damn it, we might be tired and dirty and hot and overworked, but we are still going to run this plant like a bunch of professionals." This is very easy to write, but getting such an attitude whistling through the plant along with the steam leaks is something else again. The way to develop the attitude is to play on what might be called the "Ivan Denisovitch/Oppressed Minority" quality of their existence in the plant. They work harder, longer, and in worse conditions than anyone else on the ship. Thus, they are in many ways an elite. If they can "hack the load" in an atmosphere with a mystique of elitism, and not be broken by the overall situation, then they are the best. They are proving to themselves the valuable lesson of their own strength and worth. This is the lesson that must be shown to them over and over. They are called upon frequently to divorce themselves from the home and totally dedicate themselves to the plant, especially before the major inspections. In these times, they can be appealed to on the elite basis of their situation. Let them know constantly that they do the hardest job, that it is recognized as such, and they will become the elite. They will respond as an elite group if given the identity and treated as such.

This goes hand-in-hand with the next key area of snipe leadership: *recognition*. A man will do surprising amounts of work based on the perception that he is "someone special" doing a tremendously difficult job—but he will not do it or continue to do it unless he knows someone is aware of the job and appreciates it. The types of recognition vary widely. Perhaps the best goes back to deckplate presence. When a young fireman can turn around in the bilges and reach for a wrench and find the engineer officer handing it to him asking how his job is going, legends begin to grow about that officer, and his plant will begin to work. If his only impact on the troops is an occasional well done in the night orders, he is missing the best opportunities to recognize his people. This recognition cannot come solely from the engineer officer or the other officers in the department, it must come consistently from the entire chain of command. When the BT-3, with a hard-won crow pinned on his dirty cap, can say to his detail of rube-punching firemen that they really busted to get the job done, then appreciation and recognition are really working in the plant.

The good engineer will also find ways to represent his people. As part of being aware of them and the degree of effort they put into their work, he must be ready to respond with maximum effort at his level on their behalf. He must help them in all areas including disbursing, dental, medical, civil authorities, and all the institutions of the real world that try to separate the snipes from the plant. The officer who shows up in court unasked in blues and ribbons to put in a word with the judge for one of his firemen who broke up a bar is well on the way to having his plant run well. Why? Because he is willing to put the same effort into the job at his level that he asks his firemen to do at theirs.

Awards and medals are other big items in the engineering department code of conduct for a better plant. The enlisted surface warfare expert (ESWE) pin is slanted toward the snipes, continuing the concept of "someone special." A regular program here, with officer-experts from the department available to sign off

PQS and help the candidates with bridge and CIC knowledge, is a big plus. Taking the junior petty officers, who are nearing completion of the PQS, up to the bridge and CIC and letting them conn the ship are all effective measures. One of the best junior MPAs on a West Coast destroyer, when faced with the mid-watch as OOD, would make a point of letting his junior people come up for a turn at the helm, and occasionally letting them assume the conn for simple turns. Helping them for the ESWE and even recommending them for medals and letters of commendation (when appropriate, of course) are equally good. Too many OPPE commendations are given to chief engineers when the sweat of the firemen and third class petty officers is overlooked.

The successful engineer officer will be able to make his people feel privileged. He makes them believe in themselves. And the simplest way to do that is to believe in them himself. As part of believing in them, he must be willing to accept some mistakes in watchstanders and allow them to move into positions of greater responsibility early. His reward is, ultimately, a more professional, better run plant.

When a man begins to feel that he is "someone special," doing a special, demanding job, he will respond, even in the most trying of situations. The key is to make him see himself as that individual. The effective engineer officer knows the most valuable asset in his plant: his snipe. And when he asks his people to go day after day and face the fire and the spark and the rusting pipes, he had better come ready to lead them through their own vision of themselves, from the deckplates of his own steaming world.

21 "KNOW YOUR MEN ... KNOW YOUR BUSINESS ... KNOW YOURSELF"

MAJ C. A. Bach, USA

In the November 1973 issue of *Proceedings*, retired Navy captain Alexander W. Moffat quoted extracts from an address on leadership that had been given to the graduating officers of the Second Training Camp at Fort Sheridan by Army major C. A. Bach in 1917, as they prepared for assignment overseas in what was then called "The Great War" and is today known as World War I.

His address was so well-received that it was later reprinted in its entirety on 27 January 1918 in the Waco (Texas) *Daily Times Herald*. During the next war (in November 1942), this same speech was inserted into the *Congressional Record* by Senator Henrik Shipstead of Minnesota and was also provided to the NROTC midshipmen at the University of Washington in 1943.

In a letter to the Naval Institute in early 1974, Navy captain R. C. Gilardi urged *Proceedings* to reprint it, touting it as "what is generally regarded as the best composition on 'Leadership' ever recorded." The article was reprinted in the April edition of *Proceedings* but was later also included in a special USNI publication, *To Get the Job Done: Readings in Leadership and Management* published in 1976.

"KNOW YOUR MEN ... KNOW YOUR BUSINESS ... KNOW YOURSELF"

By MAJ C. A. Bach, USA, U.S. Naval Institute *Proceedings* (April 1974): 42–45.

In a short time each of you men will control the lives of a certain number of other men. You will have in your charge loyal but untrained citizens, who look to you for instruction and guidance.

Your word will be their law. Your most casual remark will be remembered. Your mannerism will be aped. Your clothing, your carriage, your vocabulary, your manner of command will be imitated.

When you join your organization you will find there a willing body of men who ask from you nothing more than the qualities that will command their respect, their loyalty, and their obedience.

They are perfectly ready and eager to follow you so long as you can convince them that you have those qualities. When the time comes that they are satisfied you do not possess them you might as well kiss yourself good-bye. Your usefulness in that organization is at an end.

From the standpoint of society, the world may be divided into leaders and followers. The professions have their leaders, the financial world has its leaders. We have religious leaders, and political leaders, and society leaders. In all this leadership it is difficult, if not impossible, to separate from the element of pure leadership that selfish element of personal gain or advantage to the individual, without which such leadership would lose its value.

It is in the military service only, where men freely sacrifice their lives for a faith, where men are willing to suffer and die for the right or the prevention of a great wrong, that we can hope to realize leadership in its most exalted and disinterested sense. Therefore, when I say leadership, I mean military leadership.

In a few days the great mass of you men will receive commissions as officers. These commissions will not make you leaders; they will merely make you officers. They will place you in a position where you can become leaders if you possess the proper attributes. But you must make good—not so much with the men over you as with the men under you.

Men must and will follow into battle officers who are not leaders, but the driving power behind these men is not enthusiasm but discipline. They go with doubt and trembling, and with an awful fear tugging at their heartstrings that prompts the unspoken question, "What will he do next?"

Such men obey the letter of their orders but no more. Of devotion to their commander, of exalted enthusiasm which scorns personal risk, of their self-sacrifice to ensure his personal safety, they know nothing. Their legs carry them forward because their brain and their training tell them they must go. Their spirit does not go with them.

Great results are not achieved by cold, passive, unresponsive soldiers. They don't go very far and they stop as soon as they can. Leadership not only demands but receives the willing, unhesitating, unfaltering obedience and loyalty of other men; and a devotion that will cause them, when the time comes, to follow their uncrowned king to hell and back again if necessary.

You will ask yourselves: "Of just what, then, does leadership consist? What must I do to become a leader? What are the attributes of leadership, and how can I cultivate them?"

Leadership is a composite of a number of qualities. Among the most important I would list self-confidence, moral ascendancy, self-sacrifice, paternalism, fairness, initiative, decision, dignity, courage.

Let me discuss these with you in detail.

Self-confidence results, first, from exact knowledge; second, the ability to impart that knowledge; and, third, the feeling of superiority over others that naturally follows. All these give the officer poise.

To lead, you must know—you may bluff all your men some of the time, but you can't do it all the time. Men will not have confidence in an officer unless he knows his business, and he must know it from the ground up.

The officer should know more about paper work than his first sergeant and company clerk put together; he should know more about messing than his mess sergeant; more about diseases of the horse than his troop farrier. He should be at least as good a shot as any man in his company.

If the officer does not know, and demonstrates the fact that he does not know, it is entirely human for the soldier to say to himself, "To hell with him. He doesn't know as much about this as I do," and calmly disregard the instructions received.

There is no substitute for accurate knowledge. Become so well informed that men will hunt you up to ask questions—that your brother officers will say to one another, "Ask Smith—he knows."

And not only should each officer know thoroughly the duties of his own grade, but he should study those of the two grades next above him. A twofold benefit attaches to this. He prepares himself for duties which may fall to his lot at any time during battle; he further gains a broader viewpoint which enables him to appreciate the necessity for the issuance of orders and join more intelligently in their execution.

Not only must the officer know, but he must be able to put what he knows into grammatical, interesting, forceful English. He must learn to stand on his feet and speak without embarrassment.

I am told that in British training camps student officers are required to deliver ten-minute talks on any subject they may choose. That is excellent practice. For to speak clearly one must think clearly, and clear, logical thinking expresses itself in definite, positive orders.

While self-confidence is the result of knowing more than your men, moral ascendancy over them is based upon your belief that you are the better man. To gain and maintain this ascendancy you must have self-control, physical vitality and endurance and moral force.

You must have yourself so well in hand that, even though in battle you be scared stiff, you will never show fear. For if you by so much as a hurried movement or a trembling of the hand, or a change of expression, or a hasty order hastily revoked, indicate your mental condition it will be reflected in your men in a far greater degree.

In garrison or camp many instances will arise to try your temper and wreck the sweetness of your disposition. If at such times you "fly off the handle" you have no business to be in charge of men. For men in anger say and do things that they almost invariably regret afterward.

An officer should never apologize to his men; also an officer should never be guilty of an act for which his sense of justice tells him he should apologize.

Another element in gaining moral ascendancy lies in the possession of enough physical vitality and endurance to withstand the hardships to which you and your men are subjected, and a dauntless spirit that enables you not only to accept them cheerfully but to minimize their magnitude.

Make light of your troubles, belittle your trials, and you will help vitally to build up within your organization an esprit whose value in time of stress cannot be measured.

Moral force is the third element in gaining moral ascendancy. To exert moral force you must live clean, you must have sufficient brain power to see the right and the will to do right.

Be an example to your men. An officer can be a power for good or a power for evil. Don't preach to them—that will be worse than useless. Live the kind of life you would have them lead, and you will be surprised to see the number that will imitate you.

A loud-mouthed, profane captain who is careless of his personal appearance will have a loud-mouthed, profane, dirty company. Remember what I tell you. Your company will be the reflection of yourself. If you have a rotten company it will be because you are a rotten captain.

Self-sacrifice is essential to leadership. You will give, give all the time. You will give of yourself physically, for the longest hours, the hardest work and the greatest responsibility is the lot of the captain. He is the first man up in the morning and the last man in at night. He works while others sleep.

You will give of yourself mentally, in sympathy and appreciation for the troubles of men in your charge. This one's mother has died, and that one has lost all his savings in a bank failure. They may desire help, but more than anything else they desire sympathy.

Don't make the mistake of turning such men down with the statement that you have troubles of your own, for every time that you do you knock a stone out of the foundation of your house.

Your men are your foundation, and your house leadership will tumble about your ears unless it rests securely upon them.

Finally, you will give of your own slender financial resources. You will frequently spend your money to conserve the health and well-being of your men or to assist them when in trouble. Generally you get your money back. Very infrequently you must charge it to profit and loss.

When I say that paternalism is essential to leadership I use the term in its better sense. I do not now refer to that form of paternalism which robs men of initiative, self-reliance, and self-respect. I refer to the paternalism that manifests itself in a watchful care for the comfort and welfare of those in your charge.

Soldiers are much like children. You must see that they have shelter, food, and clothing, the best that your utmost efforts can provide. You must be far more solicitous of their comfort than of your own. You must see that they have food to eat before you think of your own; that they have each as good a bed as can be provided before you consider where you will sleep. You must look after their health. You must conserve their strength by not demanding needless exertion or useless labor.

And by doing all these things you are breathing life into what would be otherwise a mere machine. You are creating a soul in your organization that will make the mass respond to you as though it were one man. And that is esprit.

And when your organization has this esprit you will wake up some morning and discover that the tables have been turned; that instead of your constantly looking out for them they have, without even a hint from you, taken up the task of looking out for you. You will find that a detail is always there to see that your tent, if you have one, is promptly pitched; that the most and the cleanest bedding is brought to your tent; that from some mysterious source two eggs have been added to your supper when no one else has any; that an extra man is helping your men give your horse a supergrooming; that your wishes are anticipated; that every man is Johnny-on-the-spot. And then you have arrived.

Fairness is another element without which leadership can neither be built up nor maintained. There must be first that fairness which treats all men justly. I do not say alike, for you cannot treat all men alike—that would be assuming that all men are cut from the same piece; that there is no such thing as individuality or a personal equation.

You cannot treat all men alike; a punishment that would be dismissed by one man with a shrug of the shoulders is mental anguish for another. A company commander who for a given offense has a standard punishment that applies to all is either too indolent or too stupid to study the personality of his men. In his case justice is certainly blind.

Study your men as carefully as a surgeon studies a difficult case. And when you are sure of your diagnosis apply the remedy. And remember that you apply the remedy to effect a cure, not merely to see the victim squirm. It may be necessary to cut deep, but when you are satisfied as to your diagnosis don't be divided from your purpose by any false sympathy for the patient.

Hand in hand with fairness in awarding punishment walks fairness in giving credit. Everybody hates a human hog.

When one of your men has accomplished an especially creditable piece of work, see that he gets the proper reward. Turn heaven and earth upside down to get it for him. Don't try to take it away from him and hog it for yourself. You may do this and get away with it, but you have lost the respect and loyalty of your men. Sooner or later your brother officers will hear of it and shun you like a leper. In war there is glory enough for all. Give the man under you his due. The man who always takes and never gives is not a leader. He is a parasite.

There is another kind of fairness—that which will prevent an officer from abusing the privileges of his rank. When you exact respect from soldiers be sure you treat them with equal respect. Build up their manhood and self-respect. Don't try to pull it down.

For an officer to be overbearing and insulting in the treatment of enlisted men is the act of a coward. He ties the man to a tree with the ropes of discipline and then strikes him in the face, knowing full well that the man cannot strike back.

Consideration, courtesy, and respect from officers toward enlisted men are not incompatible with discipline. They are parts of our discipline. Without initiative and decision no man can expect to lead.

In maneuvers you will frequently see, when an emergency arises, certain men calmly give instant orders which later, on analysis, prove to be, if not exactly the right thing, very nearly the right thing to have done. You will see other men in emergency become badly rattled; their brains refuse to work, or they give a hasty order, revoke it; give another, revoke that; in short, show every indication of being in a blue funk.

Regarding the first man you may say: "That man is a genius. He hasn't had time to reason this thing out. He acts intuitively." Forget it. "Genius is merely the capacity for taking infinite pains." The man who was ready is the man who has prepared himself. He has studied beforehand the possible situation that might arise, he has made tentative plans covering such situations. When he is confronted by the emergency he is ready to meet it.

He must have sufficient mental alertness to appreciate the problem that confronts him and the power of quick reasoning to determine what changes are necessary in his already formulated plan. He must have also the decision to order the execution and stick to his orders.

Any reasonable order in an emergency is better than no order. The situation is there. Meet it. It is better to do something and do the wrong thing than to hesitate, hunt around for the right thing to do and wind up by doing nothing at all. And, having decided on a line of action, stick to it. Don't vacillate. Men have no confidence in an officer who doesn't know his own mind.

Occasionally you will be called upon to meet a situation which no reasonable human being could anticipate. If you have prepared yourself to meet other emergencies which you could anticipate the mental training you have thereby gained will enable you to act promptly and with calmness.

You must frequently act without orders from higher authority. Time will not permit you to wait for them. Here again enters the importance of studying the work of officers above you. If you have a comprehensive grasp of the entire situation and can form an idea of the general plan of your superiors, that and your previous emergency training will enable you to determine that the responsibility is yours and to issue the necessary orders without delay.

The element of personal dignity is important in military leadership. Be the friend of your men, but do not become their intimate. Your men should stand in awe of you—not fear. If your men presume to become familiar it is your fault, not theirs. Your actions have encouraged them to do so.

And, above all things don't cheapen yourself by courting their friendship or currying their favor. They will despise you for it. If you are worthy of their loyalty and respect and devotion they will surely give all these without asking. If you are not, nothing that you can do will win them.

And then I would mention courage. Moral courage you need as well as physical courage—that kind of moral courage which enables you to adhere without faltering to a determined course of action which your judgment has indicated as the one best suited to secure the desired results.

Every time you change your orders without obvious reason you weaken your authority and impair the confidence of your men. Have the moral courage to stand by your order and see it through.

Moral courage further demands that you assume the responsibility for your own acts. If your subordinates have loyally carried out your orders and the movement you directed is a failure, the failure is yours, not theirs. Yours would have been the honor had it been successful. Take the blame if it results in disaster. Don't try to shift it to a subordinate and make him the goat. That is a cowardly act.

Furthermore, you will need moral courage to determine the fate of those under you. You will frequently be called upon for recommendations for the promotion or demotion of officers and noncommissioned officers in your immediate command.

Keep clearly in mind your personal integrity and the duty you owe your country. Do not let yourself be deflected from a strict sense of justice by feelings of personal friendship. If your own brother is your second lieutenant, and you find him unfit to hold his commission, eliminate him. If you don't, your lack of moral courage may result in the loss of valuable lives.

If, on the other hand, you are called upon for a recommendation concerning a man whom, for personal reasons you thoroughly dislike, do not fail to do him full justice. Remember that your aim is the general good, not the satisfaction of an individual grudge.

I am taking it for granted that you have physical courage. I need not tell you how necessary that is. Courage is more than bravery. Bravery is fearlessness—the absence of fear. The merest dolt may be brave, because he lacks the mentality to appreciate his danger; he doesn't know enough to be afraid.

Courage, however, is that firmness of spirit, that moral backbone, which, while fully appreciating the danger involved, nevertheless goes on with the undertaking. Bravery is physical; courage is mental and moral. You may be cold all over; your hands may tremble; your legs may quake; your knees be ready to give way—that is fear. If, nevertheless, you go forward; if in spite of this physical defection you continue to lead your men against the enemy, you have courage. The physical manifestations of fear will pass away. You may never experience them but once. They are the "buck fever" of the hunter who tries to shoot his first deer. You must not give way to them.

A number of years ago, while taking a course in demolitions, the class of which I was a member was handling dynamite. The instructor said regarding its manipulation: "I must caution you gentlemen to be careful in the use of these explosives. One man has but one accident." And so I would caution you. If you give way to the fear that will doubtless beset you in your first action, if you show the white feather, if you let your men go forward while you hunt a shell crater, you will never again have the opportunity of leading those men.

Use judgment in calling on your men for display of physical courage or bravery. Don't ask any man to go where you would not go yourself. If your common sense tells you that the place is too dangerous for you to venture into, then it is too dangerous for him. You know his life is as valuable to him as yours is to you.

Occasionally some of your men must be exposed to danger which you cannot share. A message must be taken across a fire-swept zone. You call for volunteers. If your men know you and know that you are "right" you will never lack volunteers, for they will know your heart is in your work, that you are giving your country the best you have, that you would willingly carry the message yourself if you could. Your example and enthusiasm will have inspired them.

And, lastly, if you aspire to leadership, I would urge you to study men.

Get under their skins and find out what is inside. Some men are quite different from what they appear to be on the surface. Determine the workings of their minds.

Much of General Robert E. Lee's success as a leader may be ascribed to his ability as a psychologist. He knew most of his opponents from West Point days, knew the workings of their minds, and he believed that they would do certain things under certain circumstances. In nearly every case he was able to anticipate their movements and block the execution.

You do not know your opponent in this war in the same way. But you can know your own men. You can study each to determine wherein lies his strength and his weakness; which man can be relied upon to the last gasp and which cannot.

Know your men, know your business, know yourself.

22 "OUTCOMES, ESSENCES, AND INDIVIDUALS"

LT Thomas B. Grassey, USNR

It would be difficult to pass up an article that concludes with the observation that "leadership is a little like sex," but that is *not* the reason this piece was selected. Awarded First Honorable Mention in the Vincent Astor Memorial Leadership Essay Contest in 1976, this essay has much to commend it beyond that rather provocative assertion. Discounting some of the more traditional methods of approaching the study of leadership, Lieutenant Grassey concludes—in an interestingly written and somewhat iconoclastic essay—that "leadership always is given by a specific person to other particular *individuals*" (author's emphasis), and "each experience, no matter how seemingly routine, is a unique event involving individuals who defy and escape even the sagest generalizations, for ultimately it is extraordinarily personal."

"OUTCOMES, ESSENCES, AND INDIVIDUALS"
By LT Thomas B. Grassey, USNR, U.S. Naval Institute *Proceedings* (July 1976): 72–75.

It is difficult to say anything new about leadership; this field has been well plowed at least since the time of Homer and Lao-Tzu. It also seems presumptuous of one whose experience in the field is rather brief, and whose tools are so untested, to think that he will unearth some deep insight about leadership. So I won't even try. Instead, I will tell you about my individual predicament in trying to learn what leadership is, how to make it grow, and why I think the predicament has been needlessly complicated.

Though the ground has been plowed many times, and history repeatedly has shown the importance of good leadership, the new officer notices—indeed, is overwhelmed by—the tremendous swirl of confusion and contradiction about the field. In fact, explanations of leadership and advice on its improvement seem (at least to me) like dust-storms, far more confusing than clarifying, and I can't help wondering why. The harder I study leadership guides and instructions, the more obscure the subject seems to become, and the more insubstantial or vacuous the conclusions reached. The closer I look at the seemingly profound wisdom expressed in leadership essays, the less valuable it seems to be. In truth, no one is certain what comprises great leadership because great leaders vary in nearly every imaginable way. If any common qualities *are* "found" by a writer, a little scrutiny will disclose, I submit, that he has told us virtually nothing, or has begged the question by ignoring damaging exceptions, or has merely exhorted us to accept his own opinion about what qualities an ideal leader *should* possess; usually, he has done all three.

There have been two traditional standards to judge leadership, and those who investigate the literature will find these two prominent, contradictory, and (I will claim) inadequate. The first criterion of judging a leader is by the outcome of his efforts, what he succeeds in accomplishing. Thus, we say John Paul Jones, Oliver Hazard Perry, and Chester Nimitz were great naval leaders, George Washington, Ulysses Grant, and Dwight Eisenhower great Army leaders. The arbiter of greatness and the goal of leadership in war is victory (the argument runs), and they were victorious.

This approach to identifying great leadership, however, is beset with two embarrassing features: it includes figures we would like to leave out, and it excludes some we want to count in. Attila the Hun, Agamemnon, and Benedict Arnold (and some would name General William T. Sherman) were victorious, while Admiral Thomas Hart, General Robert E. Lee, and Captain Raphael Semmes were not. But the former are seldom, and the latter are sometimes, held up as model leaders. So advocates of this criterion find it necessary to modify what they mean by "success;" it now is affixed to something like "a maximum effort" or "all that was humanly possible." This change enables them to say that Lee was a great but defeated leader, while Agamemnon was a poor though victorious one. After all, the most one can do is the best with what one has, realizing that despite brilliant leadership and a supreme effort, a unit can be overwhelmed as were Leonidas' Spartans at Thermopylae. In last year's prize essay, "A Framework for Naval Leadership," Lieutenant Michael R. Svendsen adopts this attitude: "The real test of leadership lies . . . in the Performance of the group . . ."[1] Presumably, a combat unit with a great leader could achieve a collective peak effort without attaining victory. For example, writing of prisoner of war reaction to torture, Commander Robert J. Naughton observed:

> "It may be the first time in his life that he musters every ounce of physical strength, mental courage, and determination. The feeling of being totally consumed by this effort is truly unique; and even when this maximum effort, with nothing held back, proves to be not enough, one at least feels pure and satisfied for having done his absolute best."[2]

Any leader who gets this kind of "performance" from his unit must be a great leader.

Or must he? I think most of us would be uneasy saying that Adolf Hitler was a great leader, that the enormous efforts of the Russian people in World War II proved Joseph Stalin's greatness, or that the hundreds of young kamikaze pilots glorified the leadership of their commander, Admiral Masafumi Arima. Yet if one is judging leadership by "outcomes" or "the performance of the group," can one award the palm to leaders at Thermopylae and the Alamo but withhold it from Stalin and Arima?

The alternative to "outcomes" as the criterion of judging leadership has been what I shall call the "essences" approach. There are, on this view, certain essential qualities and personal characteristics of a good leader. These traits can be explained, taught, modeled, and practiced, and a fledgling like me will improve his leadership as he acquires these characteristics. Most of the *Proceedings'* essays have expressed this notion of improving leadership. One junior officer wrote, ". . . young officers, striving to develop the necessary characteristics of leadership, might well ask, 'What qualities *are* most important; where does one start?'"[3] His question was (coincidentally) answered by two other young officers quoting Admiral Arleigh Burke: "The easiest way to find what those . . . traits are and learn how to acquire them is by studying the leaders who have gone before."[4] And a Navy captain is willing to help us out on this subject: "Today, a leader needs the timeless motivational qualities of leadership, or he will never taste success. What are some of these qualities?"[5]

Before considering the nominees the captain proposes, could we pause for a moment to really think about his first quoted sentence (which is typical of much of the leadership essay genre)? "Today, a leader needs . . . leadership." Ah, very good, very true, but *not* very helpful. "The timeless"—*are* leadership qualities timeless? Maybe some are, but certainly few of those he gives us fit that adjective. "Motivational"—is this redundant? I mean, if *anything* is timeless, that leadership means motivation of others would seem a safe bet. "Or he will never taste success"—if this is history, or statement of present fact, or even prophecy, it is transparently false. Many successful leaders were, are, and will be lacking (egregiously lacking) in "self-discipline, patience, loyalty, humility, understanding, attention to detail, organization of effort, singleness of purpose, consistency, and total honesty" that the captain specifies as "*some*" of the "timeless motivational qualities of leadership."

This recommendation to study leadership exemplars as the way to improve one's own leadership is based on an assumption which is false, or meaningless, or circular. If it means that great leaders share some important qualities, X, Y, and Z, which few other persons possess, it is false. In truth, what one sees when one follows Admiral Burke's advice to scan history for the unique elements common to great leaders is *nothing*. Some are meticulous, some casual; some punctilious, others anti-ritualistic; many physically strong, a few chronically ill; a number intellectually brilliant, most just average; and so on in every identifiable respect. If humility is required of great leaders, men such as Raymond Spruance qualify but those like John Paul Jones do not. Lee was a model of bearing, courtesy, and sobriety—quite unlike his counterpart and equal as a leader, Grant. Dan Gallery was the soul of impish, irrepressible humor; Ernie King prided himself on being "an S.O.B." Eisenhower and George Patton are highly esteemed as leaders, but what qualities did both display that today's junior officer could emulate?

If one still insists that, despite glaring exceptions, great leaders of the past generally exhibited traits which we should acquire, the statement verges on emptiness. What the advice amounts to, it appears, is that by looking back through history we will see that great leaders were, in fact, great leaders. Since there is—so far as I can see, at least—no significant constellation of traits hovering above history's leaders, what more this is to suggest is unclear.

If, however, an "essentialist" on good leadership were to say, "Look, here are some men who most certainly *were great leaders*, and they in fact *did* have features in common; I'd suggest you study them to learn what those traits are," it appears quite circular. *Why* were those individuals selected? If it was because they had certain wonderful traits, and I agree that they are wonderful traits, then I don't need to study the men to find the traits, do I? As General Eisenhower remarked, "For people who like this kind of book, this is the kind of book they will like." If Patton is your idea of a great leader, your great leaders will be a lot like Patton. But suppose I think Patton was a megalomaniac? If you think great leadership is marked by boldness and the flair for the dramatic and I don't, you'll enjoy William Halsey's biography more than Spruance's and I won't. Or I could point out that Hitler was bold to invade Russia, and Hideki Tojo's order to attack Pearl Harbor was dramatic. But you would not read their biographies for leadership lessons, would you? An essentialist, you see, already knows what a great leader is before he goes looking to find out. And of course we *describe* phenomena to fit our preconceived judgments: "I am consistent; you are stubborn. I am cautious; you are hesitant. I am humorous; you are a buffoon. I made an honest error; you made a foolish gaffe. . . ." "Obliteration bombing of German cities was to break civilian morale and shorten the war; V-weapon attacks on London were terror tactics." "Jonathan Wainwright's Corrcgidor surrender was honorable to avoid a futile loss of life; Lloyd Bucher was 'pusillanimous.'"

As a final remark on essentialism, why have the "Comment and Discussion" pages of the *Proceedings* reverberated with sniping and defensive fire on Admiral King's leadership? Surely not on the basis of the Navy's "performance!" No, it is about his title to greatness; and quite a few *admirals*—even though they knew him well—disagree strenuously on whether this man had the characteristics of a great leader. Likewise, Admiral Elmo Zumwalt's leadership has been both widely hailed and notoriously bewailed. If there are some definite leadership traits that junior officers can identify and acquire, why are senior officers (whose very careers have required leadership for 30 years) unable to recognize, agree on, and apply them?

Most of the writing one finds on leadership is exhortative, because moral values are packed into the definitions of "leadership." If we are talking simply of getting a job done, psychologists and sociologists can provide tons of relevant data. Few essays on leadership cite such findings, however, because the authors do not want to call certain ways of getting a job done "leadership." If you really want to collectivize farms, almost nothing that has appeared in the leadership essays, for instance, will be of much value. Why? Because those writing about leadership (and/or those selecting articles for publication) assume that a real leader must exhibit admirable moral features. Many essays in this field, consequently, have a distinct "Boy Scout" flavor because of their fervent idealism. There is nothing wrong with this so long as it is recognized as an opinion about what the words "good leadership" should mean. There is something quite wrong, though, if one believes one is making a *factual* report, telling us that leaders are successful because they are humble, loyal, completely honest, etc. Such efforts at "objectivity" and "the straight factual scoop on great leadership," are almost worthless.

In addition to suggesting that essays which pretend to be factual when they really are pep talks probably don't do much good (though they make us feel a little better about ourselves and our leadership), I will venture further and say they do some harm in hiding what leadership really is and distracting us with fruitless attempts to develop "leadership traits."

"What is a leader?" and "How can I be a better one?" are simple, worthwhile questions with unsurprising but continually forgotten answers. A leader is someone who is followed. You can be a better one if others have greater reason to follow you. I'm sorry, but that's all there is. Perhaps it could be noted, though, that the answers are *true* (virtually by definition) and *non-judgmental* (no moral presupposition is involved). Even the question of whether *being* a leader is good is left open. Leadership itself is amoral. A good leader can bring out our human capacity for villainy as well as for nobility. A group out for a mutiny or gang-rape may not be your idea of a leadership opportunity; but it is there, and the unsurprising answers about leadership apply exactly as in the more familiar case studies on the subject.

What reason do people have for following someone as a leader? They want to go where he is leading ("want" in the broadest possible sense, conscious or subconscious, from positive incentives like a desire for glory to negative inducements such as fear). What does this imply for our efforts to become better leaders? At least that an alternative to the "outcomes" and "essences" approaches to studying leadership is required.

"He knew something that none of the rest of us knew," William Golding wrote in *Free Fall*. "He knew about People." The reason young officers usually are rather ineffective leaders isn't because they lack certain "traits" (which they could acquire by exercises in character development); it is because they do not yet know much about people. The main cause of a newly-commissioned division officer's awkwardness in leading his senior petty officers is that he has experienced nothing at all like this in his life! All his "singleness of purpose" and "knowing his stuff" cannot really alter the fundamental oddity of a 22-year-old novice "leading" older, more experienced, dedicated professionals. He has little idea how such men will respond to him.

One reason white officers of any rank find it harder to lead black, chicano, Filipino, American Indian, and other minority sailors than middle class white youngsters is because we know so relatively little about them. As simple a thing as a "yassuh" of a certain volume, intonation, and inflection confuses us; we know what middle class white disrespect sounds like, but we just aren't sure whether this minority sailor is "sassing" us. So even in the most mundane interactions we are less comfortable with him.

To cap this off, almost all young men and women are still learning vast amounts about themselves. We are not completely sure who we are, where we are going, what we will value, and what we expect of others. This rather inhibits (or *ought* to inhibit) our readiness to say, "Follow me!"

The main drawback to leadership training on the "outcomes" or "essences" models is, I believe, that it misrepresents what it is doing, and thereby misleads us about what *we* should be doing. That needs explanation. "Outcomes" and "essences" pretend to be giving factual information, some objective truths about leadership. In reality, they are value judgments, prescriptions, and recommendations. They tell the young officer how he should perceive and present himself; they focus on him. "If you behave in this and this and this way, you will be a good leader." "To improve your leadership, study how David Farragut, Thomas Truxtun, and Marc Mitscher acted, and imitate them." This approach to leadership is, I submit, radically misguided if not downright bass-ackwards.

It certainly helps to know who you are and where you are going, but that sort of knowledge seldom is acquired through hearing a lecture or reading an essay on leadership. Examples and experiences, not words, are the real teachers of values. "What you are thunders so loud," Ralph Waldo Emerson wrote, "that I can't hear what you say." Even though young officers may not be completely sure of their identities and goals, it is most improbable that they can be *told* these things. In fact, to encourage imitation and, to some extent role-playing and posturing seems precisely the worst possible advice to give a maturing individual who most needs to experience authenticity and self-acceptance.

But more importantly, the emphasis is on the wrong place. It is indisputable that we best learn about ourselves from interactions with others. So instead of focusing on ourselves and our own "techniques," I suggest we should learn about the individual men and women we are to lead. To be better leaders (whether we wish to lead men for good or for evil), we need to know more about *those whom we want to follow us*. What are their backgrounds? Why are they as they are? What are their dreams, aspirations, vulnerabilities, and fears? How can they be motivated? This is the diametric opposite of most leadership essays, because the focus of this kind of training as a supplement to experience is on the *individuals we are to lead* rather than on ourselves. We could study biographies of past leaders to understand *them* as individuals (rather than collections of leadership "traits"); but even so, I think any officer wanting to improve his leadership today would be better advised to read Gerald Messner's *Another View: To Be Black In America*, Stan Steiner's *La Raza*, or Dick Gregory's *No More Lies*. You will never have to command David Farragut or Chesty Puller (about whom you probably already know quite a lot), but you are right now responsible for leading men about whom you know terribly little.

Finally, leadership always is given by a specific person to other particular *individuals*. Why Smith followed your leadership yesterday may or may not be why Johnson will (or will not) follow it today. As we have noted, the best way to learn about ourselves is from interacting with others; and the most practical way to improve our leadership is to know more about those we want to follow it. This implies that our own day-to-day leadership successes and failures—with all their attendant details right before us for careful study—are the best heuristic devices for improving our leadership. As Saint Exupery's Little Prince was told: " 'Then you shall judge yourself,' the king answered. 'That is the most difficult thing of all. It is much more difficult to judge oneself than to judge others. If you succeed in judging yourself rightly, then you are indeed a man of true wisdom.'"

In conclusion, leadership is a little like sex: One whose only knowledge of the subject is from a "how to" manual and lectures is a poor participant; one who reads about the experiences and techniques of others might be a little—but only a little—better. For proficiency, doing it is far better than reading about it; different folks need different strokes; and knowing very well the person with whom you are doing it allows you to do it about as well as you can. If you really want to improve your skill, the best way is to try to understand what you did right the good times and wrong the bad, which requires honesty about yourself, intimate knowledge of the other, and frank communication. Still, each experience, no matter how seemingly routine, is a unique event involving individuals who defy and escape even the sagest generalizations, for ultimately it is extraordinarily personal.

Notes

1. Lieutenant Michael R. Svendsen, USN. "A Framework for Naval Leadership," *Proceedings*, July 1975, p. 22.
2. Commander Roberts J. McNaughton, USN. "Motivational Factors of American POW's Held by the DRV," *Naval War College Review*, January-February 1975, p. 7.
3. Lieutenant Bruce Stuart Lemkin, USN. "The Current State of Leadership in the United States Military: No Crisis Here," *Proceedings*, October 1975, p. 84.
4. Lieutenant R. T. E. Bowler, III, USN, and Lieutenant D. R. Bowler, USN. "The Naval Officer: Manager or Leader?" *Proceedings*, December 1975, p. 67.
5. Captain F. C. Collins Jr., USN. "The Loss of Leadership," *Proceedings*, April 1975, p. 33.

23 "DISSIDENCE IS NOT A VIRTUE"

ADM Arleigh Burke, USN (Ret.)

The open exchange of ideas (frequently referred to as "the open forum") provided by the Naval Institute through its magazines, books, oral histories, and seminars is frequently hailed as one of USNI's greatest strengths. To be effective, such a forum must of course include a willingness to criticize as well as provide useful information and support for those ideas deemed beneficial. Sometimes viewed as anathema by those whose vested interest is the subject of criticism, true believers in democracy understand and applaud this important but sometimes painful function.

As an illustration of that forum in action, we can review this article written by Admiral Arleigh Burke and published in the April 1976 issue of *Proceedings*. The article itself does not offer a great deal to the dialog on leadership, but the responses that it engendered are noteworthy, not only for the ideas they contain but as relevant examples of this forum that has been cherished, protected, and effective for nearly a century and a half.

Despite the high rank and well-deserved iconic status enjoyed by former chief of naval operations and World War II hero Arleigh

Burke, there appeared, in several subsequent issues of *Proceedings*, rebuttals to his piece.

Beginning with Admiral Burke's article, we see what might be classified as a senior officer's view of leadership, or at least one aspect of it.

"DISSIDENCE IS NOT A VIRTUE"

By ADM Arleigh Burke, Chief of Naval Operations, 1955–1961, U.S. Naval Institute *Proceedings* (April 1976): 78–79.

In reading the leadership prize essays published in the *Proceedings* during the last year, I have noted that several of our young officers have commented on the examples set by past and present leaders. But the tendency has been to mention only those at the very top, not the business of junior-senior relations in general. Much of the growth to leadership as a senior is to be a good follower as a junior, so I thought it might be well to spend some time discussing that point.

I think I and all people around my time wholeheartedly accepted the Navy as an ordered organization which required that we work within a framework of authority. We were imbued with respect and admiration for our seniors. When we were young we realized our seniors knew more than we did, that they had experience—worthwhile experience—which we did not, and that they were better naval officers than we were. We wanted to become like the people who had gone before us, and we tried to follow the example of the better ones. Certainly we knew that some of our seniors were not very good. Some of them had grave defects. And we did not want to become like some of the poorer officers. But even the poorer officers frequently had more knowledge in some fields than we did—and some characteristics that were admirable. We tried to pattern ourselves after those seniors we admired and respected the most. We tried to pick up and develop the characteristics that we thought we should have.

Certainly we did not feel we knew more than our seniors, that we knew we could run the ship, the unit, or the Navy better than our seniors, even when they did make mistakes and sometimes did something obviously foolish. It was apparent to us that the promotion system was pretty good. The best officers were usually selected, and the poorer ones were not. We knew that the selection system worked pretty well. For example, about the time we were lieutenant commanders we used to make lists of those officers we knew whom we thought the selection board should pick for captain or rear admiral. It was surprising how similar our lists were to those of the selection board. Once in a while we thought somebody had been selected when much better qualified men were available, but that was infrequent. Usually we believed that the people who were selected were among the best qualified officers. In short, we had faith based on our observation of the system, a system which worked pretty well—not perfect, but pretty good just the same.

Of course we knew the Navy could be improved, and every once in a while some youngster had an idea of how that could be done. He talked it over with his peers, and he discussed it with his boss. Sometimes the senior agreed—but more often he did not. That was because usually the bright idea was not as good as the originator thought it was, including a lot of my own ideas. If we were not convinced our senior was right we would try again, but we usually did not go outside the chain of command. When someone was found by-passing the usual procedure, it was all too frequently a man who was seeking personal aggrandizement, although this was not always so. We had confidence in the fairness of the authority within which we worked. We felt that our seniors—and our juniors—were trying to make the Navy better, and so we were encouraged to express our ideas for the good of the ship and the service.

Changes were made slowly, perhaps too slowly, but they were made and carried out without disruption. In the last century Admiral J. A. Dahlgren developed a new type of naval gun. He was an impatient man and was greatly frustrated and disgruntled by the action of a senior Navy board or committee which did not accept his concept right away and start manufacturing his guns. The board—or whatever—kept asking him for more data and fuller explanations, and Dahlgren, who could see the Civil War coming, believed the men on the board were simply trying to thwart him in his efforts. Dahlgren was furious, but all he could do was try to convince what he apparently thought was a stupid bunch of old fogies that his concept was worth putting into practice right then. The board wanted tests. How could it be loaded? How would it work on a rolling and pitching platform? Was the gun strong enough, might not it blow up? Was it too heavy, etc.? Well, he made tests, and, in the process, he improved his design. Even so, one gun did blow up, and there were casualties.

The point is that all the roadblocks that Dahlgren was so sure were unnecessary forced him to improve his design until it did work. I doubt if he ever realized—he certainly did not say so if he did—that his gun was made successful largely because his design and concept were questioned by an experienced bunch of old duffers.

Of course, views of younger people should be listened to and considered. But many proposals are not sound—even those from experienced people. The best ones must be tested. Not all proposals can be tested. There's not enough time or money. Judgment comes from experience. If the senior officers in the Navy are wrong frequently, then our whole system is wrong, and the experience a man gets as he works in our profession is wrong. I don't think the whole system is wrong. We made a lot of mistakes in World War II, but not as many as any of the other nations did—so I think our system was pretty sound. At least at that time it worked, and it worked better than others—and now do we discard it at our peril? I think most of the seniors in the Navy have pretty good judgment, although I am forced to admit that I shudder sometimes at some of the actions taken. Still I don't know the circumstances under which those judgments were made. Those decisions I think were wrong may have been made by a senior with faulty concepts or faulty judgment. If so, the system slipped that time when that individual was selected to a senior rank, but that does not mean the system has fallen apart. It does mean it can be improved, and it should be.

Dissidence is not a virtue. Experience is not worthless. Good judgment is necessary, and good judgment comes from experience and study of what has happened. The rules and regulations of an organization are never perfect, but action must be taken within those rules, or chaos and uncertainty result. The SOP's cannot be changed abruptly without disruption and confusion.

Diversity of views and opinions are necessary, too, but they must be carefully and calmly presented and considered on their merits. Frequently, there is no clear answer, and all participants must realize—or be forced to accept—the truism that nobody is endowed with all knowledge or prescience. {Comment and Discussion. *Proceedings* (July 1976)}

Editor's Note

Three months later, the following letter appeared in the July 1976 issue of *Proceedings* as a "Comment and Discussion" (C&D) feature. In it, Commander Chirillo agrees with Admiral Burke's basic premise but contends that there have been instances of "intelligent judgments that led to acts, against orders, which saved situations." He allows that there are times when a "commander is suddenly possessed of knowledge that his superior's planned objectives can only be achieved by disobeying." While this is not exactly mutinous thinking, it is still a bit eye-opening, not only in what is advocated (imagine such a letter appearing in a Soviet or North Korean publication), but also with whom the writer is disagreeing.

Commander L. D. Chirillo, U. S. Navy (Retired)—Certainly dissidence is not a virtue, and experience is not worthless. Experience is the essential substance of the U. S. Navy Regulations, a "framework of authority" which has endured the test of time. Good judgment does come from "experience and study of what has happened." It also comes from intelligence. History also describes intelligent judgments that led to acts, against orders, which saved situations.

Perhaps the best known is Nelson's departure from the single-line ahead during the Battle of St. Vincent. With sound judgment and promptitude he abandoned his superior's battle plan in order to cut off an escape open to most of the enemy.

A better example simultaneously involved all ranks from captain to ensign. It relates to the tragic losses sustained by Destroyer Squadron 11 in 1923 when two of its three divisions followed their leader through fog onto the rocky coast near Point Arguello, California. The squadron commander's critical navigation order was based upon a position judgment derived from dead reckoning. It was reviewed by three division commanders and 13 destroyer commanding officers. Experienced navigators were apprehensive but did not object to the order. Discerning action was initiated by only two ensigns in the trail division's flagship. They found it necessary to by-pass their skipper in order to report their fears to the division commander, who was known to be a strict disciplinarian. The latter secured a margin of safety by directing a shift to seaward and opening the distance between his flagship and the ship ahead. His division was spared.

The subsequent Court of Inquiry, Courts Martial, and comment by observers and naval historians have addressed the conflicting requirements of the destroyer doctrine to follow-the-leader and each unit commander's responsibility to assure the safety of his unit. Extremely simplified, it appears that most agreed that safety of a unit is paramount—except during wartime in the presence of an enemy as a superior's basic plan must be followed, unless a unit commander is suddenly possessed of knowledge that his superior's planned objectives can only be achieved by disobeying.

Minds boggle at the thought of the confrontations that are possible. Complications are introduced by the fact that in peacetime naval officers are preoccupied with learning how to evaluate wartime risks. But their decisions for like risk situations must sometimes be different in peacetime than in war.

Thus, intelligent obedience is a virtue. Its value is not likely to be described better than in an opinion shared by Vice Admiral Charles A. Lockwood U. S. Navy (Retired) and Colonel Hans Christian Adamson in their book, *Tragedy at Honda*:

> Placing absolute faith and confidence in a leader has been both a curse and a blessing since the dawn of history. It has led to the rise of despots and dictatorships; it has led to the creation of free nations, such as ours; it is the foundation of all religions. Again the dividing line must be drawn by common sense, conscience and evaluation of the end to be attained. No leader or ambition should ever be followed blindly unless the risk has been carefully calculated. In war calculated risks are matters for everyday consideration. {Comment and Discussion. *Proceedings* (August 1976)}

Editor's Note

The following month, another C&D letter appeared; this one takes on Admiral Burke even more directly, ultimately concluding that the problems that dissidence may bring are potentially offset by the possibility that "fallible policies" may not be "exposed to the test of war."

Captain Brian R. Jackson, U. S. Naval Reserve—Subordination, essential as it is, can no longer be considered, in the post-Nuremberg world, as an absolute virtue; but even less can dissidence (which my dictionary defines as "disagreement") be considered an absolute vice. Few would disagree that we badly need the "diversity of views and opinions" of which Admiral Burke speaks. But we cannot secure the benefits of such views without allowing their expression, including expression of disagreement with established policy. It does not suffice to assert that dissent within the "system" is allowable, but that dissent outside the system is not. For if dissent was truly tolerated within, there would be no need to proscribe its practice without. The problem is that dissent, even inside the system, is considered to be more or less insubordinate. This is inherent in the system as we all know but occasionally overlook. If we really want the benefit of dissenting views, their expression must be unequivocally freed from the stigma of insubordination. Of course, a line must be drawn between expressions which merely criticize the policies of the system and those which attack and threaten its integrity. As in our civil society, the distinction may not always be clear-cut. But I believe that if our system is truly sound, "chaos" and "confusion" are not inevitable consequences of attempting this. Perhaps we might suffer the discomfiture of finding that a doctrine or policy cannot stand the test of contrary ideas, but this would be a small price indeed compared to the price exacted when fallible policies are exposed to the test of war. {Comment and Discussion. *Proceedings* (November 1976)}

Editor's Note

Again, the following November, another C&D letter appeared, this time by another admiral. While he understandably includes a caveat that makes clear his appropriate deference ("I hesitate to criticize some of the basic statements made by an officer with the experience and qualifications of Admiral Burke"), he nonetheless offers his disagreements and alternatives, while making clear the importance of not only his thoughts but the open forum itself.

Rear Admiral Charles Adair, U. S. Navy (Retired)—I agree with Admiral Burke that criticism should be through channels and should relate to constructive suggestions. Two points which I question, however, are the title, "Dissidence Is Not A Virtue," and the statement that "The SOPs cannot be changed abruptly without disruption and confusion."

I hesitate to criticize some of the basic statements made by an officer with the experience and qualifications of Admiral Burke. But the very fact of my hesitation makes me wonder if junior officers reading this article might not be deterred from taking future action, or positions contrary to general opinion, because of a strict adherence to the basic positions outlined in this article. While there were modifications stated in the article, these may be forgotten in the future.

I have been fortunate in my duty assignments in the Navy, because, almost without exception, I believed that I could provide contrary recommendations to my superiors and that such recommendations would be considered in the same spirit in which they were offered.

As one who has always encouraged those with whom I worked to come up with a better idea if they had one, I will outline a few differences of opinion which I have sponsored in the past. In this way, I may clarify my points.

In 1955, when I was on duty in the office of the Navy Comptroller, a question arose about a major change in financial reporting desired by the Secretary of Defense. The Assistant Secretary of the Navy called five of us to a meeting on this subject, which we knew he favored. After some discussion, the secretary said, "Let's see how you all feel about it." He asked each of us in turn and everyone said, "No, don't do it."

The secretary leaned back in his chair and laughed loudly saying, "Well, at least I don't have a bunch of 'Yes' men."

It is easy to agree, or to keep quiet, particularly when you know that you have the only contrary opinion. But I have always believed that, when appropriate, I should present my honest opinion and take the consequences. To do otherwise is a failure to support properly those for whom you work.

In 1943–1944, I headed the planning section for the Seventh Amphibious Force which was responsible for General MacArthur's assault operations. One of our early operations was the assault on the Admiralty Islands. This assault cut off, from the rear, the main Japanese base at Rabaul and gained control of the best harbor in the Western Pacific.

Air reconnaissance indicated that there were few, if any, Japanese troops in the area of the proposed landing. A quick meeting was called by the Army of all the forces involved, and it was there that the Navy first heard of the assault. The basic plan for a reconnaissance in force with about 840 troops came by dispatch from General MacArthur to his Army Ground Force Commander who called the meeting.

The plan was quickly outlined and was approved by the Commanding General, by the Army Assault Force Commander, by the Army Air Forces Commander, and then the question was asked of Admiral Barbey, Commander Seventh Amphibious Force. He said, "I would like to hear what my planner thinks;" and he turned to me in the rear of the room, "Charlie, what do you think of this plan?"

I had no information regarding this assault before this meeting, but our planning group received copies of 41 photographs taken in the southwest Pacific area by the Army Air Forces. These arrangements were made as soon as I joined the staff because, frequently, with only two or three days to get out an assault plan, our planning group would not have time to receive new intelligence reports. I remembered pictures of Los Negros Island which related to this operation.

I stood up and said: "I don't like the operation. We should not land on the southeast end of Los Negros because of the coral reefs near the surface and the coral shelf above will make it very difficult for the boats to unload. Also, I don't like the jungle behind this landing area. There is something wrong there but I don't know what it is."

"We should land inside Hyane Harbor at the north end of the airstrip where there is a good sandy beach. It is only about two miles to the north. We should also send in two LSTs, which will not delay the landing, but will allow us to land about 2,200 troops together with tanks, guns, and ammunition which we may need."

Admiral Barbey commented, "I like your assault plan better." So did the others in the meeting, and it was agreed to use the new plan. A short time later, however, the Commanding General Ground Forces modified the plan back to the original one, except that he retained the new assault beach which I had recommended.

The assault went off as planned. Later information showed the coral to be as described at the southeast end of Los Negros. In the jungle behind that beach, however, were a five-inch gun and 403 Japanese troops. Nearby, but across a small inlet were 2,000 additional troops. At the beach to the north, where we landed, the rapid resupply of our troops, together with a destroyer off the beach for gunfire support for two days, prevented the defeat of our landing force.

The basic strength of the American people is their inherent initiative and common sense. Of course in any organization, civilian or military, there must be direction to ensure that initiative is channeled into areas for the common pod. But in measuring suggestions, it is well to keep in mind a statement by "Mark Twain" who said, "The man with a new idea is a crank until the idea succeeds."

I would like always to encourage initiative and new ideas for without them the military, as well as civilian business, would stagnate.

For this reason, I would like to offer a new title for Admiral Burke's article: "Without good judgement and common sense, dissidence is not a virtue."

CONCLUSION

To reiterate (and emphasize) a point made in the introduction to this book, what appears here is nowhere near the complete corpus of leadership-related information that has appeared in Naval Institute venues over the many years of its existence. Readers may well know of other qualifying pieces that were omitted. The sheer size of this body of work stands as testament to the importance of the subject and, as already noted, its elusiveness.

The quest is not over. Until someone somehow captures the essence of leadership in a single, all-inclusive, undeniable, and completely convincing work, the quest will continue. But it is reassuring to know that the U.S. Naval Institute will continue to provide the forum that is essential to such a quest.

INDEX

accountability, 143
Adair, Charles, 191
Adamson, Hans Christian, 189–90
adaptability, 98
Adelman, Ken, 10
administrative leadership, 53–61
Admiralty Island assault, 192–93
Agamemnon, 175, 176
Alexander the Great, 65
amoral leadership, 180–81
Another View: To Be Black In America (Messner), 182
Architecture of Leadership (Phillips and Loy), 3
Arima, Masafumi, 176
Arnold, Benedict, 175
Athens, Art, 13
Attila the Hun, 175
attitude formation, 20
authority: decentralization of, 99; delegation of, 25; as extraordinary measure, 2
aviation pipeline selection, 119
award presentations, 104, 161

Bach, C.A., 163
Bacon, Francis, 65, 66–67
Barbary Wars, 150
Barbey, Daniel E., 193
Battle of St. Vincent, 188
battle readiness, 36
Bennis, Warren, 10
Bluejackets Manual, 83, 86
Bonaparte, Napoleon, 72, 106
Bowler, D.R., 31, 54
Bowler, R.T.E., 31, 54
bravery, versus courage, 172
Bucher, Lloyd, 179
building blocks of leadership, 13–14
Burke, Arleigh, 40, 177; on dissidence, 185–88; on leadership development, 41–42

can-do spirit, 98
Captain's Mast, 106–7
Career Compass (Winnefeld), 113
Carlson, E.F., 71
case-study method, 3
Cassius, 65

chain of accountability, 143
"chain pulling" syndrome, 80
"Challenge to Navy Management, The" (Korth), 34
character development, 48–49
charismatic leadership, 53–61, 74
Chaucer, Geoffrey, 43, 52
Chief Petty Officer Initiation, 69
chief petty officers, 117–18, 127; division officers and, 134–38. *See also* enlisted personnel
Chirillo, L.D., 188
Churchill, Winston, 3, 8
coercive power, 24–25
collective punishment, 105
command indoctrination, 141
command presence, 96
Commander William Earl Fannin, Class of 1945 Capstone Essay Contest, 145
commanding officer: in establishing leadership approach, 58; micromanagement by, 77–78; in setting priorities, 75
commissioning programs, 118–20
communicating the "big picture," 86
communication, open, 76
communication skills, 92, 97
compassion, 92
competence, 74
confidence, 90–91
Conrad, Joseph, 133, 143
consistency, 74–75, 84, 103
convincing, as leadership approach, 30
cooperative thinking, 95
correspondence course completion, 105
counseling skills, 146–47
courage, 92–93, 95, 125, 171–72

Cribbin, James J., 34
crisis management, 75
criticism, 78–79
Cutler, Thomas J., 5, 81

Dahlgren, J.A., 186–87
Day of Infamy (Lord), 1
decisiveness, 91
deckplate leadership, 160
decoration presentations, 104
delegation of authority, 25
department head, 137, 139; enlisted personnel and, 155; leadership traits of, 151–56; as mentor, 155
Department Head Schools, 152
dependability, 49
deployment issues, 147
Destroyer Squadron 11, 188–89
direct orders, 142
disassociated tour, 120
discipline: basis of, 102–3; characteristics of effective, 103; consistency in, 74–75; good example in, 49; in Marine unit, 95; Pearl Harbor attack and, 1–2; purpose of, 102
disciplining, 105–6, 169
dissent: as disruptive, 187–88; toleration of expression of, 190–91; tradition of loyal, 127–28
division chief petty officer: developing relationship with, 134–37; in junior officer development, 137–38; strengths and weaknesses, 138–39
division officers, 132; basic counseling by, 146–47; chief petty officer relationship with, 134–38; department head mentoring of, 155; enlisted personnel and, 140–42; junior, 133;

reciprocal respect and, 64; supporting subordinates, 130–31; ten commandments for, 142–43
Division Officer's Guide (Noel), 5, 35
division officer's notebook, 125–26
division space tour, 135
Drill and Ceremonies Manual, 104
duty, 66–67, 95

education, 97, 116
Effective Managerial Leadership (Cribbin), 34
egoistic needs, 22
Eisenhower, Dwight D., 9, 175, 178
Emerson, Ralph Waldo, 181
endurance, 91
engine-room leadership, 157–62
enlisted evaluations, 149–50
enlisted personnel: command indoctrination and, 141; counseling of, 146–47; department heads and, 155–56; direct orders and, 142; distractions and job performance, 147–48; division officer and, 140–42; educational levels of, 140; engine-room crew, 157–62; leading as "whole persons," 125–26; maintenance of prerogatives and, 76; Marine, 98–100; petty officer leadership, 81–86, 127; racial minorities, 180–81; reciprocal respect and, 64, 117; recognition for, 161; supporting, 130–31; warfare qualifications, 161–62
enlisted promotions, 104
enlisted surface warfare expert (ESWE) pin, 161–62
equipment management, 154
Erskine, Graves B., 97

essences approach in evaluation, 176–77
essentialist approach to evaluation, 178–79
Estes, Kenneth, 94
Everyday Leader Heroes, 70

Fannin, William Earl, 145
Fiedler, F.G., 18
1 Corinthians 14:8, 112
fitness report expectations, 128
flexibility, 91
Fliegel, Robert A., 73
follower-leader contract, 30
followership, 85–86, 90, 127–28
following up, 156
forcefulness, 92
forehandedness, 76–77
forward thinking, 127
"Framework for Naval Leadership, A" (Svendsen), 176
Fraser, Powell, 56
fraternization, 86, 99, 170–71
Free Fall (Golding), 180
French, J.R.P., 24

Gallery, Dan, 178
Gates, Thomas, 64
gentlemanly attributes, 48–49
genuineness, 123
Gilardi, R.C., 163
Golden Rule, 83–84, 128
Golding, William, 180
"gotcha" syndrome, 80
Grant, Ulysses S., 175, 178
Grassey, Thomas B., 54
Gregory, Dick, 182
group-oriented leaders, 17, 24

Halsey, William, 178
Handbook of Leadership (Stogdill), 16
Hardy, Thomas Masterson, 62–63
Hart, Thomas, 176
hierarchy of needs, 21–22
Hitler, Adolph, 176, 178
honesty, 72, 124
human nature in leadership theory, 20–21
humility, 68–70, 72, 126, 178
"hurry up and wait" syndrome, 77

IG inspections, 110
individual needs, 18
initiative, 91–92
innate traits, 12
inspections, 107–10
integrity, 89, 125
intuition, 72

Jackson, Brian A., 190
Jefferson, Thomas, 150
Jones, John Paul, 40, 64, 88, 175, 178
Journal of a Lifetime, The (Pleat), 70
Judeo-Christian ethics, 45
junior division officer, 133
junior officer career advise, 115–19
justice, 92, 171

Kacher, Fred W., 121, 151
King, Ernest, 178, 179
Korth, Fred, 34
Kotter, John, 10

La Raza (Steiner), 182
Le Terrible (Spain), 63
leader: function of, 16–17; identification of potential, 23

leader orientation, 17
leadership: as amoral, 180–81; authority and, 2; defined, 2–3, 9–10, 35, 54, 71; "essences" approach to evaluation of, 176–77, 181; importance of, 11; individual nature of, 4–5; innate versus learned, 12; outcomes criterion in evaluation of, 175–76, 181
leadership and management training (LMET) school system, 59
leadership approach: assessment of, 175–77; charismatic versus administrative, 53–61; commanding officer in establishing, 58; convincing others as, 30; current problems in, 27–28; debate concerning, 3–4; leading the "whole person," 125–26; Marine Corps', 15–16; of snipe-capable officers, 159–62; task- versus group-oriented, 17
Leadership (Burns), 3
"leadership by walking around," 135–36
leadership development: Arleigh Burke on, 41–42; charismatic-administrative paradigm, 59–60; current problems in, 27–28; division officer in providing, 148–49; in peacetime, 39–40; research on, 23; structure of, 23–24
Leadership Development Continuum, 93
leadership development programs (LDP), 93
leadership effectiveness factors, 16–17
Leadership Embodied (USNI), 5
leadership learning process, 12–14
leadership paradigm, 33

leadership principles, 24
leadership theory: contradictions in, 175; human nature as factor in, 20–21; on leadership training, 23; need satisfaction in, 17–22; traditional assumptions in, 16; value systems in, 20–21
leadership traits: ability to communicate, 92; adaptability, 98; of administrative leader, 55; of charismatic leader, 55; compassion, 92; competence, 74; consistency, 74–75, 84; courage, 92–93, 125, 171–72; decisiveness, 91; of department head, 151–56; dependability, 49; difficulty of emulating, 177–78; duty, 66–67; endurance, 91; in engine-room, 157–62; essentialism in identifying, 178–79; fairness, 92; flexibility, 91; followership, 127–28; following up, 156; forehandedness, 76–77; honesty, 72; humility, 68–70, 72, 126; innate versus learned, 12; integrity, 89, 125; intuition, 72; liberal knowledge, 65; loyalty, 72, 89–90, 117, 143; maintaining prerogatives, 76; of Marine Corps leader, 96–98; maturity, 90; in military leader, 164–73; moral leadership, 92, 166–67; open communication, 76; in petty officers, 81–86; positive attitude, 92; praise giving, 78–79, 84, 169; preparedness, 169–70; prioritization, 75; professional knowledge, 63, 85, 88–89, 97, 142–43, 153, 165–66; punctuality, 99, 122–23, 129–30; resilience, 77–78; self-confidence, 90–91, 165; setting a good example, 49, 84, 96, 122, 124, 143, 167; taking responsibility, 84; taking the initiative, 91–92; will, 90
leadership versus management, 10–11, 32–40; in civilian sector, 34–35; compatibility of approaches in, 36; shipboard duty and, 37–38; system efficiency and, 44; in wartime, 38–39
"Leading the Leader" (Fraser), 56
Lee, Robert E., 173, 176, 178
Lejeune, John A., 43, 50–51, 96
Lincoln, Abraham, 3
Little Prince, The (Saint-Exupéry), 182
Lockwood, Charles A., 189–90
Lord, Walter, 1
loyal dissent, 127–28
loyalty, 72, 89–90, 117, 143

Maier, N.R.F., 20
management: civilian versus military managers, 36–37; defined, 34–35; versus leadership, 3–4, 10–11, 32–40; in wartime, 38–39
management by objectives, 75
management paradigm, 32
manager development, 33–34
Marcus Aurelius, 71
Marfiak, Thomas E., 61
Marine Corps Manual, 51
Marine Officer's Guide, The, 94
Marshall, S.L.A., 43, 49
Maslow, Abraham, 22
maturity, 90
McComas, Lesa A., 87
McGregor, Douglas, 15, 20
McLean, Ridley, 81, 86

Meditations (Marcus Aurelius), 71
men-money-materials triad, 34
message drafting, 78
Messner, Gerald, 182
micromanagement, 85; by commanding officer, 77–78
midshipmen advice, 114–20
midshipmen essay contest, 145
military bearing, 128
military leadership, 71, 164. *See also* leadership
Minerve (Britain), 63
mission accomplishment, 26, 128
Mitscher, Marc, 63
model method of study, 3
Moffat, Alexander W., 163
Montgomery, Bernard, 9
moral courage, 171–72
moral leadership, 92; character development in, 48–49; foundations of, 43–52; in military institution, 51–52; in modern society, 50–52; rights and responsibilities in, 48; self-confidence as factor in, 166–67; self-improvement in, 50
moral revolution, 45
motivation, 21
Murphy, Jm, 68

natural law, 47
Naughton, Robert J., 176
naval culture, 129–31
"Naval Officer, The: Manager or Leader" (Bowler and Bowler), 54
Naval Officer's Guide, 49, 87
naval planning, 126
Naval Terms Dictionary (Noel and Beach), 2–3

Naval War College, 39
Navy General Order 21, 9, 54
need satisfaction: individual and organizational, 17–22; leader's role in, 22–23, 23–24, 72; measure of effectiveness in, 26–27; as motivator, 21–22; reciprocal respect in, 62–64, 66
needs of individuals, 18
negativism, 77–78
Nelson, Horatio, 62–63, 188
Nevada (USS), 1
Newly Commissioned Naval Officer's Guide (Kacher), 121
Nimitz, Chester, 175
No More Lies (Gregory), 182
Noel, John V., 35
non-attribution of orders, 79

obedience, 189, 190
office hours, 106–7
officer promotions, 103–4
O'Hara, Michael J., 43
open communication, 76
open forums, 184, 195
Operation Enduring Freedom, 156
operational competence, 123–24
operational culture, 130
opinion development, 22
orders: direct, as rarity, 142; in emergency situations, 170; issuing and enforcing, 100–101; undermining through non-attribution, 79
organizational needs, 19
"Outcomes, Essences, and Individuals" (Grassey), 54
outcomes criterion in evaluation of leadership, 175, 181

patrol aviation, 119
Patton, George S., 100, 178
Pearl Harbor attack, 1
Perry, Oliver Hazard, 175
personnel management. *See* management
"Perspectives on Leadership" (Tyler), 29
Peter Principle, 74
petty officers: division officer and, 135–36; leadership traits in, 81–86. *See also* enlisted personnel
philosophical morality, 46–47
physical courage, 172
physical readiness, 97, 167
pipeline selection, 119
planning skills, 126, 153
Pleat, George, 70
positive attitude, 92
power basis, 24–25
praise giving, 78–79, 84, 92, 169; occasions for, 103–4
preparedness, 169–70
Preparing to Lead (Athens), 13
prerogative maintenance, 76
Princeton (USS), 156
prioritization, 75
Proceedings magazine, 5, 68, 163
professional knowledge, 63, 85, 88–89, 97, 128, 142–43, 153, 165–66
Professional Naval Officer, The: A Course to Steer (Winnefeld), 132
professional standards, 160–61
promotion ceremonies, 103–4
promotion system, 186
pulling rank, 101–2
punctuality, 99, 122–23, 129–30
punishment, 105–6, 169

"Qualifications of a Naval Officer" (Jones), 40

racial minorities, 180–81
"rank has its privileges," 101–2
Raven, B., 24
reciprocal respect, 62–64, 169
reenlistment ceremonies, 105
reference guides, 131
referent power, 24–25
religious morality, 46–47
reprimands, 105–6
reputation, 114–15
Request Mast, 106–7
"Requirement for Exemplary Conduct" (Navy Regulations), 45
resilience, 77–78
responsibility: assuming, 84; centralizing, 99
retirement ceremonies, 105
Rickover, Hyman G., 55
rights and responsibilities, 48
road marching, 103
role reversal, 83–84
Rommel, Erwin, 98–99, 100–101

safety needs, 22
Schuttler, Rich, 69
scientific management, 33
self-actualization needs, 22
self-assurance, 95
self-confidence, 95, 165
self-discipline, 90, 102–3
self-edification process, 4–5
self-improvement, 50
self-knowledge, 88, 182–83
self-sacrifice, 167
Semmes, Raphael, 176

servant leadership, 150
service reputation, 114–15
service selection, 119
setting the example, 49, 84, 96, 122, 124, 143, 167; through good followership, 85–86
Sherman, William T., 175
shipboard leadership, 11; in leadership versus management paradigm, 37–38
Shipstead, Henrik, 163
snipe leadership, 159–62
social media, 29, 141
social needs, 22
Socrates, 43, 46, 112
special request chits, 76
special warfare officers, 119
SPOM learning model, 13–14
Spruance, Raymond, 178
staff work, 154
Stalin, Joseph, 176
Stavridis, James, 53, 157
Steiner, Stan, 182
Stogdill, Ralph M., 16, 23, 25
subordinate development, 98–100
subordination, versus dissidence, 190–91
Surface Warfare Officer Schools, 64
Svendsen, Michael R., 176
systems efficiency, 44

tactical action officer (TAO), 152
tactical performance, 128
task-oriented leaders, 17, 24
temper tantrums, 79, 90, 105
Ten Commandments for career development, 115–19
Ten Commandments for division officers, 142–43

Theory X and Y, 15, 20–21, 26, 27
threat making, 79
To Get the Job Done: Readings in Leadership and Management (USNI), 163
Tojo, Hideki, 178
Tragedy at Honda (Lockwood and Adamson), 189–90
Truman, Harry S., 9
truth telling, 124
Twain, Mark, 194
Tyler, David, 29

undersea warfare simulator, 152
Uniform Code of Military Justice, 105
unlawful order, 100
U.S. Army, 9
U.S. Civil War, 186
U.S. Coast Guard, 9
U.S. Constitution, 48
U.S. Marine Corps: devotion to, 98; inspections, 107–10; leadership approach in, 15–16, 18; leadership traits in, 96–98; organizational needs in, 19; subordinate development, 98–100; wartime leadership, 95–96
U.S. Marine Corps' leadership training program, 27–28
U.S. Naval Academy, 145
U.S. Naval Institute, 5, 29, 68; essay contest, 41; open forums provided by, 184, 195; speaker programs, 39
U.S. Navy Regulations, 45

value systems: in leadership theory, 20–21; moral revolution in, 45–46; sources of, 46–47
Vincent Astor Foundation, 41

Vincent Astor Memorial Leadership Essay Contest (VAMLEC), 41, 43, 53, 61, 174

Wainwright, Jonathan, 179
Walker, Frederic John, 142
"walking around leadership," 135–36
Wall, Thomas U., 15
war-fighting competence, 123–24, 154
warfare qualification, 116, 161–62
wartime management, 38–39
Washington, George, 175
watchstanding culture, 130
weapons proficiency, 110–11
Welch, Jack, 154

Wheel Books series, 5–6
will, 90
Winnefeld, James A., Sr., 113, 132
Winter, Robert Van, 145
work/life balance, 150
World War I, 163
World War II, 1, 187, 192–93
Wray, Robert O., 7

Xenophon, 66

"yes men," 192

Zumwalt, Elmo, 179

ABOUT THE EDITOR

Thomas J. Cutler has been serving the U.S. Navy in various capacities for more than fifty years. The author of many articles and books, including several editions of *The Bluejacket's Manual* and *A Sailor's History of the U.S. Navy*, he is currently the director of professional publishing at the U.S. Naval Institute and Fleet Professor of Strategy and Policy with the Naval War College. He was awarded the William P. Clements Award for Excellence in Education (military teacher of the year) at the U.S. Naval Academy and is a winner of the Alfred Thayer Mahan Award for Naval Literature, the U.S. Maritime Literature Award, and the Naval Institute Press Author of the Year Award.

The Naval Institute Press is the book-publishing arm of the U.S. Naval Institute, a private, nonprofit, membership society for sea service professionals and others who share an interest in naval and maritime affairs. Established in 1873 at the U.S. Naval Academy in Annapolis, Maryland, where its offices remain today, the Naval Institute has members worldwide.

Members of the Naval Institute support the education programs of the society and receive the influential monthly magazine *Proceedings* or the colorful bimonthly magazine *Naval History* and discounts on fine nautical prints and on ship and aircraft photos. They also have access to the transcripts of the Institute's Oral History Program and get discounted admission to any of the Institute-sponsored seminars offered around the country.

The Naval Institute's book-publishing program, begun in 1898 with basic guides to naval practices, has broadened its scope to include books of more general interest. Now the Naval Institute Press publishes about seventy titles each year, ranging from how-to books on boating and navigation to battle histories, biographies, ship and aircraft guides, and novels. Institute members receive significant discounts on the Press's more than eight hundred books in print.

Full-time students are eligible for special half-price membership rates. Life memberships are also available.

For a free catalog describing Naval Institute Press books currently available, and for further information about joining the U.S. Naval Institute, please write to:

Member Services
U.S. NAVAL INSTITUTE
291 Wood Road
Annapolis, MD 21402-5034
Telephone: (800) 233-8764
Fax: (410) 571-1703
Web address: www.usni.org